Only A Mother
The Demarion Pittman Story

by Edna Pittman

This book is dedicated to my mother Elsa Smith. Your love and support have carried me thus far. Your prayers have sustained me. I know I will never experience a love like yours in this lifetime. I pray I can give my children exactly what you gave me, a mother who loves them unconditionally. Thank you for leaving your imprint on my heart. Rest In Paradise.

Deja, Destini and Demarion, my world didn't become complete until each one of you entered my life. I thank God He chose me to love you.

Contents

Chapter 1: A Mother

Train up a child in the way he should go: and when he is old he will not depart from it.

Proverbs 22:6 (KJV)

I always knew I wanted to be a mother. I don't mean while I was playing with my baby dolls as a child. I mean, I knew I wanted little people to raise, just like my mother raised me. I wanted girls and boys. I think I had baby names picked out by the time I was 12. As a child, I enjoyed each moment with my mom. She was always willing to spend time with me, teach me and love me. She was the person I looked up to. She was the person I wanted to be just like. I grew up knowing she would do anything for me, and she would never let anyone hurt me. I knew she had my back, but would let me have it if I was in the wrong. She taught me how to be a little girl. She taught me about cleaning, cooking and reading. My mother is the person who taught me how to pray. I wanted to be a good mother just like her. I wanted to guide children, teach them to be good citizens. I wanted them to make a difference in the world. My mother believed in everything I ever wanted to do. She even made me do things I didn't want to, like taking acting classes, singing in front of the church, and enrolling me in debate and speech. Before I ever knew what I would do with my life, my mother prayed and asked God to show her what I would be and how she could help me reach my purpose. Now that's a good mother. I wanted to be the same kind of mother, but I always told myself I wouldn't drag my kids to church every time the doors were opened. Although I wanted to be just like her, little did I know that her love and her life would guide most of the experiences in my life.

It was no surprise that I had children. I loved children, although I wasn't sure whether I did when I worked at my grandparents' daycare center as a teenager.

Some of those kids made me question why anyone would even have children. My first daughter was born in my second year of college. Although I was unwed and my mother was furious with me, she stuck by me and guided me during that scary journey. She insisted I eat right and take vitamins. She wanted to know about all my appointments, even when I was mad at her and didn't want to speak to her. On the day my daughter was born, I had a regular checkup. It didn't take the doctor five minutes to tell me I had preeclampsia, and they would have to induce labor. I was scared out of my mind, and all I wanted was my mommy. As the nurse guided me to a phone so I could call her, to my surprise she walked right through the door. I couldn't believe it. How did she even know I was here? She had seen my car in the parking lot and figured I had an appointment. She told the receptionist who she was, and they led her to my room. In case I hadn't mentioned this, my mother is a praying woman, so there was no doubt in my mind that God sent her to be there with me, even before I knew I needed her. She helped me with every aspect of our little darling Deja. Sometimes I thought she forgot I was the child's mother and thought she was.

When my second child was born, also a girl, I was married. It had been five years since my first child. My husband and I had moved to a city more than an hour away. We were determined to do things on our own. We went to the hospital late that night, and several hours later our little Destini was born. The first person we called was my mother, and although it was before the crack of dawn she was excited. She was the first person at the hospital that morning so she could hold her newest grandbaby. She stayed with me for two weeks after Destini was born. She didn't let me lift a finger. She let me rest, and she took care of everything. When it was time for her to go, Tim and I actually wanted her to stay because we had been spoiled.

Two years after Destini was born, I found out I was

pregnant again. I thought I had the flu for about two weeks before I realized it might be something else. The day I took the test, I knew in my heart that I was pregnant. I wasn't working outside the home at the time, and Tim and I had talked about having another child because we wanted a little boy, but I sure didn't think this would be the time. Sure enough, the test was positive. I figured I would break the news to Tim lightly, so I cooked dinner, and after he ate I told him. He just looked at me and said good, maybe it will be a boy. I thought he was going to be upset, but he wasn't at all. He smiled and told me everything would be okay. This third pregnancy was horrible. I'd never been so sick in my life. We had one car, so I took Tim to work each day. I can't remember how many days I had to pull over just so I could throw up. I was miserable. I spent countless days in the hospital because my blood pressure was high or the baby wasn't moving enough. When I had the first ultrasound, Tim couldn't bear to go because he was scared it was going to be another girl.

With all that was going on, my mother constantly called and prayed. She would send me money and buy things for the girls and the new baby. She made sure Tim and I didn't stress too much, because she knew there was no way I could work. The day my third child was born, I was miserable. I had labored all through the night at home. I didn't want to be in a hospital for a long time because I had the girls, and I didn't want anyone to have to watch them for me.

When I finally told Tim I thought it was time, I called the hospital and told them I was on my way. The nurse told me they had no room, so I would have to go to another hospital. I couldn't believe it. By this time my contractions were only a few minutes apart, and I wanted to kill someone. Tim was so calm as he took his time loading the kids in the car, dropping them off to our friend and driving the speed limit to the hospital. By the time we arrived, I really wanted to run him over with the car. Once we got to the hospital and checked in, they rushed me to a room.

I hadn't been in the room more than fifteen minutes when my mom walked in. I couldn't believe it. I hadn't called her to say I was on my way to the hospital. I hadn't even talked to her that day. She was smiling and so excited. Tim and I were shocked because she didn't even live in the same town. She told us she was at a church in town and decided to stop by the house. When she realized we weren't there in the middle of the day, she called my best friend and asked if she knew where I was. She came to the hospital (this all must have been before the HIPAA laws), and they gave her the room number. She had made it just in time to witness the birth of her grandson, Demarion.

My mother taught me what a mother should be. A mother loves her child no matter what. She supports her children and helps them in any way they can. She even showed me that a mother can love you but tell you when you are wrong. I learned from her that only a mother can feel when something big is going to happen. She feels the pain her children feel, and she prays them through anything that comes their way. As my mother, she prepared me to be the mother I am today.

Chapter 2: Daily Prayers

It's a day I'll never forget. I can remember it like it was yesterday. It's a day I don't want to forget, because it's the day my life changed. I was just an average girl born and raised in Oklahoma. I had earned a degree in broadcast journalism and had been a reporter and producer, and now I was a television director for the federal government. It was a life I had chosen, because commercial television didn't fit the lifestyle I wanted with three young children. I was happily married to Tim for six years now, and we were doing okay. We were getting ready to start looking at houses to purchase our first home. So, "normal" is exactly how I would have described my life.

August 2, 2007. When I wake up each morning, I pray for my children. I always prayed for my children, but today the prayer was just a little longer. I also prayed that I would be the best mother possible to my children, just like my mom. It started out as all my days during the summer did. I tried to sleep in as long as I could, because I didn't have to take my oldest two children to school. Instead, they would go to daycare, along with their baby brother, Demarion. We were all still trying to recover from the trip we had just made to Disney World days prior. We had just had the most fabulous vacation to Orlando. Our entire family was there for a family reunion. Demarion was the youngest of the great-grandchildren and kept us all laughing. He was either wanting someone to pick him up or being a little rascal! He almost gave Tim a heart attack when he jumped into the swimming pool with no warning. Tim can't swim. While at the Magic Kingdom he had a ball until we went to a show that had bears. He cried so much Tim had to take him out. We couldn't believe how scared he was considering how much he terrorized everyone around him. He never seemed scared of anything, and there didn't seem to be anything scary about the show.

We had also had a huge breakthrough with his potty

training. Over the past several months, we had been working so hard to get him trained. Yet after one session with my mother and his cousin Jadon, he was trained! My mom took Demarion into the restroom with Jadon so they could both go to the potty. Jadon was a year older than Demarion. Once Jadon began to go, my mom said Demarion had this look of astonishment on his face and just did what he saw Jadon doing! We were so excited. If I had known that was all we had to do, I would have had Jadon show him sooner! It was great because the rest of our trip Demarion went to the potty like a big boy.

I finally dragged myself out of bed and began to start my day. Although I hesitated getting out of bed, I knew I would need to get things rolling, because I had an 8:30 staff meeting. I got my two oldest girls up and advised them to get dressed, wash their faces and brush their teeth. It was our morning ritual. My oldest Deja, 10, would get her sister Destini, 5, and head toward the bathroom. It was known in our house not to disturb Demarion, because at 3 he was a night owl. Ever since I could remember, he refused to fall asleep before midnight, sometimes walking around the house in the middle of the night while the rest of us slept. The girls got dressed, and I checked to make sure Destini had decent socks because they were going on a field trip with the daycare center. They were going bowling, and I refused to let her go with anything less than a perfect pair of socks.

The girls were pretty much together, and it was time to get Bari ready. Bari was the name Destini gave Demarion when he was born because she couldn't pronounce his name correctly. I woke him with the usual kiss, and he turned over as if to tell me to leave him alone. I continued to get him dressed as he slept. He looked so cute in his new Tommy Hilfiger shirt and khaki shorts I had just purchased from the outlet we visited in Florida. I even managed to brush his teeth while he was asleep. He did

10

manage to wake up to let me know he did not want to wear the Nikes I had out for him. Instead, he wanted to wear a pair of Elmo shoes my mother had bought for his third birthday. Although they did not match, I didn't feel like that fight this morning. I figured I would give him a break since he had been a big boy and went to the potty by himself.

I made sure I had the money for the field trip in an envelope to give to Mrs. Alexander when the kids arrived. I told my husband goodbye; he had just gotten in from work and was in the bed. We dropped off Deja at the school daycare. She didn't attend the same center as the younger two because the school offered a program that allowed her to be with children her age. I watched her get into the classroom and headed to daycare. Mrs. Alexander had been watching the kids for about six months. I chose her out of six other centers that I called or visited. She was a Christian woman and offered everything I wanted for Destini and Bari—homework help, field trips and lots of learning. Destini and Bari loved it. It was a diverse home daycare center, something that was important to me. I trusted this woman, and she had never given me any reason to feel that she did not have my children's best interests at heart. She was a mother, and I could tell she loved all the children in her care. She informed me on everything that happened daily.

I pulled up to the house and realized I couldn't park in the driveway because there was lumber all over the place. Mrs. Alexander had mentioned she would be adding on to her home. As I got the kids out of the car, Demarion began to fuss. He was still tired and didn't want to be bothered. He was halfway eating a Pop-Tart and threw it. We made it to the door, and as always, Destini was excited to start the day at daycare. She went in, found a bean bag and began watching cartoons. Demarion on the other hand was being his usual mean self. I was excited to share

Demarion's potty training success with his caregiver, because she had been working with him also.

Mrs. Alexander's husband was sitting next to the television. He would watch the kids some mornings while she was getting ready for the day. He said hello and reached for Demarion. Demarion wasn't having it. I let him down, and her husband reached again and said, "Hey man, come on. Mommy has to go." Immediately, Demarion kicked him. I wish I could say I was shocked, but I wasn't, because that's the kind of little boy he was. I knew he liked her husband, but he was still sleepy and this type of behavior was typical. But that didn't mean I was going to let it slide. I'm a firm believer in respectful children, and even at age 3 and sleepy, Demarion was going to get in trouble for his actions. I immediately got down to his level, popped his little leg once and made him apologize. Did I mention my son was also extremely stubborn and looked at me like I was crazy? He wouldn't say a word, so I put him in the timeout chair and told him he was to stay there until Mr. Alexander said otherwise. I gave him a kiss and headed out the door. As I left, I couldn't do anything but laugh because he was such a mess. I never thought that would be the last time I saw him that way.

My day had gone great at work. I had been worried about my dental insurance coverage, so that afternoon I decided to walk to Human Resources to see if someone could explain it. No one was in the office, so I headed back to my office. It felt nice outside, so I took the long way back. It was after 3 p.m., and I was getting hungry, so I stopped at the break room at the end of the hall in my building. I picked up a candy bar and headed back to my office. As I reached the door, Kristy asked me where hers was. I showed her that the one I had was filled with almonds, which she didn't like. I was standing at her desk talking about the wedding she was planning when my cell phone rang. I saw that it was Mrs. Alexander. I remember thinking, "Why would she be calling me at 3:15 when I get off in about an hour?"

I answered the call, and the voice on the other end sounded pretty calm. "Edna I need you to come to my house right now. There's been an accident." Immediately my heart dropped. "What kind of accident?" I asked. "Demarion has been hurt. He was left in the car." All I could say was, "Is he ok?" Again she said, "I need you to come to my house right now." I dropped the phone. By this time Kristy could tell something was extremely wrong. She picked up the phone. "Who is this?" was the last thing I remember her saying. I ran to my cube and grabbed my things.

My office lead, Rich, said, "What's wrong Edna?" I explained that the daycare center called and said Demarion had been left in the car and I needed to go. Kristy came to the back and tried to help me get things together, but I was absolutely hysterical. I couldn't remember how to get in contact with Tim. I couldn't remember my mother's phone number. I couldn't remember a thing. Rich then took the phone and called the daycare center. He was told they were transporting Demarion to the OU Children's Hospital and for us to go there. Kristy and I immediately ran out of the office. We got in her car, and although I could barely breathe, I remember her saying, "Put your seat belt on. It's going to be a bumpy ride." That it was indeed. I'm sure my friend broke more traffic laws than I care to mention. She took me to Tim's job, because he only worked a few blocks from our office. She pulled up, jumped out of the car and ran in. I sat in the car praying; asking God to please let Demarion be okay.

When Kristy came back, she said Tim was on his way. I managed to call Stacie, my best friend of 15 years and Demarion's godmother. I felt horrible for asking her to meet me at the hospital because her son had died in the same hospital a year ago. I knew she wouldn't want to be anywhere near that place, but I also knew that I really needed her there with me. The hospital was more than fifteen minutes away, but I swear Kristy got me there in five. We arrived, and she dropped me off at what we thought was the emergency room entrance but turned out to not be. There was no one in sight, and no signs to tell me where to go. I walked down a long hall and finally ran into a nurse. I explained I was looking for my son who was being brought into the ER, and she told me I was in the wrong building. I guess she could tell I was in no condition to take directions and make it to the ER by myself. She told me she would take me. She calmly asked why he was coming to the ER. I told her that his daycare center had called and said he had been left in the car and was hurt. She got me to the right building, and I went to the counter. The clerk had no idea who Demarion was. I then heard over the scanner that they were in route. I left the ER and waited outside. Kristy had parked and came to stand with me. I then saw Stacie walking across the street with Jeremiah.

Kristy had phoned my parents, and they were on their way. By this time my cell phone was ringing off the hook. Family members were calling to find out what was going on.
A fireman pulled up, parked and came to where we were. He asked if I was the parent of the little boy left in the car. I said, "Yes, is he ok?" He told me he didn't know. He was sent to pick up one of the men who were riding in the ambulance with Demarion. He assured me they were on their way. As the ambulance pulled up, I remember wanting to run to it, but I knew I couldn't get in the way. I saw them pull my little boy out on the stretcher with all sorts of things hooked up to him. The look on their faces told me it was extremely serious. They asked if I was his mother. ." They said just follow us. It was like my feet couldn't move. I had never been so scared in my life. I said "Bari, Mommy's here." He didn't respond as we were

running into the ER.

Immediately, doctors and nurses began working on him. People were asking me more questions than I had ever been asked at once. Is he allergic to anything? What do you call him? How much does he weigh? At that moment I couldn't remember my own name let alone the answers to some of these questions. I was in shock. That morning I left my healthy, full of life, stubborn and precious little boy at a daycare center to care for him, and now I was here. It truly felt like an out-of-body experience. Never in a million years could I have imagined this. If I could have turned back time, I would have, but I couldn't. I was in a whirlwind of uncertainty.

"Why is it taking Tim so long?" was the only thing I could think. It seemed liked I was in this room alone. At that moment I needed my husband. God knew I needed him there, because he called and asked me where we were. He was at the hospital, but in the wrong wing. He rushed over and when he made it to the ER, he was speechless. I had never seen this look of fear and anger on my husband's face. The paramedics began asking Tim and me questions about insurance, but all I could do was focus on what they were doing to Demarion. I saw a lady standing outside the room with the police, and I remember thinking it must be social services.

The public relations officer for the hospital approached us. He told us the media was all over the story since Demarion was hurt at a daycare center. They wanted interviews. We both immediately told him no media were allowed. We had both been in the commercial television business and knew what they were doing. At that moment I understood why people want privacy.

People were coming at us left and right, question after question. I could tell by the looks on their faces that they too were scared and devastated for our son. My husband was enraged, and I was afraid he might snap, but he didn't. He managed to keep it all together. Again, the look on his face told me exactly how he felt.

Chapter 3: The Fight Begins

Doctors finally told us it was a miracle that Bari was even still alive. They explained everything they wanted to do to him, some of which was extensive and frightening. They had hooked him up to several things and had to get our permission to do whatever they thought possible to save his life. They advised us that he was in critical condition and said they had no idea what the outcome would be. They prepared us for the worst. They advised us they didn't know if he would make it through the afternoon, let alone the night.

The Chaplain came in and asked if we wanted him to pray with us. I told him yes, because at that moment the only thing I knew to do was pray, but I didn't have the words to say a prayer. I was completely numb. After the chaplain prayed, I remember the feeling that came over me. It was a feeling of calmness. Something told me I had to be strong and that Demarion would live. I couldn't explain it. I had this feeling that this was bigger than me, and I had no control over what was going to happen. It was the hardest thing for me to grasp. At that moment, I knew only God was in control of this situation. I could only ask him to spare my son's life. I said a silent prayer. God, please let Demarion live. He's my baby, my only son. I'm not sure I'll be okay if he doesn't survive. Lord, I know there is nothing I can do, but I gave Demarion back to you when he was a baby, and now I'm asking you to let me keep him.

I had had all of my children dedicated to the Lord, because as their Mother I understood that God had given me these children. He had given me these precious gifts to raise and teach them about him. He had entrusted me to help them reach their purposes in life, which would ultimately glorify God and do his will. At that moment, I didn't feel Demarion had served his purpose in life, so I couldn't let go of him.

The medical staff had worked on Bari for more than

an hour. I know because my parents and grandparents live more than an hour away and my mother came walking in the room. I will never forget how she looked and how she prayed. She immediately went to Demarion and began to pray. My mother was a praying woman. She had always prayed. She prayed more than anyone I knew. Growing up, she taught my sister and me how to pray. She prayed over us when we were asleep. She prayed for us when we were angry with her. She prayed for us as adults. She prayed for her grandchildren. My mother was strong in her faith. She knew about the healing power of God firsthand. She had been battling cancer and prayed her way through it. I had no idea how she was able to get into the room. They had told us only Tim and I could be there. I later found out she asked no questions and just came through the doors. She needed to pray for her grandson, and no one was going to stop her. Tim later told me he saw her as he was coming back from being interviewed by Child Protective Services. He said a nurse tried to tell my mother she couldn't go through the doors, and he had asked the nurse to please let her go.

Bari barely made a sound. His eyes could barely move. There were tubes all over him. His breathing was shallow, and the tube going down his throat was the worst thing I could have imagined for my baby. I couldn't stop wondering how this had happened to my child. He was an innocent little baby boy. He was full of life, and in an instant it seemed like his life was being taken away from him. I kept wondering whether he realized what had happened. Did he cry for help from his Mommy and Daddy, and we weren't there? Was he awake in that car? Did he suffer and realize no one was going to save him? Did he wonder why his sisters were not around to help him?

We had just taken a trip to Disney World three days prior. Demarion had just turned three. We thought he would love seeing all the characters he watched on television, but he was terrified of most of the larger-than-life characters. Tim told me he kept saying "Daddy" and would hide his face. Tim hated the look on Demarion's face, because he knew he was truly frightened. That's the look Tim never wanted to see again. He was our protector. He was the man that Demarion looked up to. He knew his Daddy would keep him safe. It tore Tim apart to know that he wasn't there to protect or prevent Demarion from this horrible accident.

It was my turn to talk to Child Protective Services. They asked me questions about the daycare center. They wanted to know if the kids ate well while they were there. They wanted to know if we noticed anything bad about the center. I couldn't believe it. I was not the kind of parent to leave my children with people who were not responsible. I wanted to say check her track record. I did before I enrolled my children. I would have never imagined this could have happened while they were in her care. She was always loving and nurturing with all the children. She seemed to be very attentive to their needs and wants. She was always staffed with enough people to help with the amount of children I saw in the center. She seemed to take an interest in each child. She taught them. She played with them. She encouraged them and worked to help each child meet his or her potential. Her center was featured in a commercial for the governor's wife. She had a diverse center and had been recognized for her great strides in childcare. This was the kind of center where parents wanted their children. I had taken my children out of several centers for things that some would say were petty. They were my children. I had to work, and I wanted them to be with someone who could do the job of caring for them in the manner I would if I were able to stay at home. I politely answered their questions and asked what was going to happen. The social worker advised me there would be an investigation, and they would let me know the results.

Once I returned to the room that Bari was in, I knew it would be a long night. Doctors and nurses were discussing his condition with police and my husband. At that moment I only wanted to be near my baby. I had to let him know I was there, and I would not leave him. I felt if he just heard my voice he would be okay. I began telling him I loved him, and he was going to be okay. He never responded. He just made a moan. Not one time did I cry. I'm not sure why. I guess it was the shock. I guess I felt that if he knew I was crying he would be scared. When we would play and I would act as if I were crying, he would get upset. I knew Demarion didn't like for me to cry. He had been through enough today. The last thing he needed was his mother crying, screaming and falling out everywhere. If I couldn't be strong for myself or my family, I was going to be strong for him. He was a fighter. He had been since he was in the womb. It was now my turn to fight for him.

Doctors told us they had him stable enough to move to the next stage. He was going to a room in the Pediatric Intensive Care Unit (PICU). They told us he was not out of the woods, but they couldn't keep him in the ER. They kept telling us it was a miracle he was making it to the PICU. They told us most kids are found dead in the sweltering cars they are left in.

Demarion was transferred to his room. That was the first sign of hope for me. I thought God couldn't let him die. His little life had just begun. He still had too much to do. I needed to show him so much more love. I needed to raise him, be a mommy to him and believe in him.

The nurse gave us a long list of instructions about the unit and the room. She said no more than two people could be in the room at a time. I listened because I knew I needed things to be as simple as possible.

By this time co-workers and more family had

arrived. My family from Texas had made it to the hospital in record time. I can't tell you how much it meant to have so many people loving and encouraging us. They prayed with us. They cried with us. They hung in there with us. Deja was at the afterschool summer program. LaToya, my sister, picked her up. She explained to Deja what happened. Next they would pick up Destini from the daycare center. It never crossed my mind that it might be a bad idea because my sister has a temper and might hurt Mrs. Alexander . Fortunately, she was still in shock and didn't want Deja to see her act up. Later she told me she even asked Deja if she wanted to go in the house to get Destini. Deja told her no, she was too upset with what had happened.

We didn't have the girls come to the hospital that day because things were so hectic and Destini had seen enough. I spoke with them both on the phone. I tried to assure them that Demarion would be just fine, although I had no idea what the outcome would be. I was surviving on faith at this moment. Nothing but faith and hope were keeping me on my feet. I tried not to let them know I was scared, hoping they wouldn't be scared if I was strong. I worried about Destini and what she saw. How would she handle this? I didn't want her to feel it was her fault. My father and stepmother made it that night. My dad didn't tell his wife right away what was going on, because she loved her grandbabies and he didn't want to immediately upset her.

While I thought this had been the hardest day of my life, I was wrong. Sleep wasn't an option for Tim and me. We found out sleep was somewhat overrated for a few weeks.

That night was awful. Neither of us wanted to close our eyes in fear of the unknown. We shared a chair next to Demarion's bed. The nurse brought us blankets, and Tim insisted that I try to get some rest. He's always been the night owl. I was the one in bed by 10 p.m. every night. I had always been that way. My mother would tell stories of how I would act if my sleep schedule was off. This night it wasn't a problem. It was so hard to fall asleep. Each time I doze off, something would wake me. If it wasn't the lights, nurses or sounds of machines, it was the mere feeling of something being absolutely wrong. I would awake only to realize it had not been a dream. My baby was in fact fighting for his life. It felt so awful. It is a pain I will never be able to describe. Nothing has ever hurt so much.

Chapter 4: Pray and Wait

The next morning, the doctors made their rounds. They came with students telling them about Demarion's case. This bothered me, but I didn't say anything. I knew this was a learning hospital. All I really wanted to know was what they could tell me about Demarion. Would he be ok? When would he wake up? He had made it through the night, so that must have meant something good, I thought. Well, I was wrong. Not only could they not tell me much, but they had nothing good to say. They continued to tell us they weren't sure he'd even survive. They continued to tell us we might need to prepare for his death. This confirmed the nightmare that I was in. It was a nightmare that I couldn't wake up from. At this point, all I could do was pray and hang on to the faith I had in God. I had faith God wouldn't give me more than I could handle. I had faith he was hearing my prayers and the prayers of so many people across the nation.

My cell phone rang so much from people all over the United States. People I hadn't heard from in years. People I didn't know. I began to wonder how they got my phone number. I then realized it didn't matter. They were praying for my baby. They were praying for my family. Since there had been no change in Demarion's condition, the head doctor requested a CAT scan. He needed to know what was going on in Demarion's head. When the results came back, they explained that his entire brain had swollen. What this meant was severe brain damage. They explained there wasn't much they could do to relieve the swelling because it was the entire brain. This was not the type of news I was hoping and praying to hear. Why? Why my son? He was an innocent little boy who hadn't hurt a soul. He didn't deserve this. Then I thought... no one, no child deserves something like this to happen. At that moment, I decided not to question this accident anymore. I would never wish this to happen to any child. I began to focus on what we were facing and what I could do to help my baby.

It had been two days, and I still couldn't grasp what had happened. It was too overwhelming. I immediately needed to be around the girls. I needed my family together, not apart. They needed me as well. They were hurting just as much as Tim and I were. My mother insisted that I eat, but I couldn't. Eating was the furthest thing from my mind. How could I eat when my baby couldn't eat? It felt awful. I knew I needed strength, but it just didn't make sense. How does a mother eat at a time like this? I kept hearing it over and over: Eat! I finally managed to take down a couple spoonfuls of mashed potatoes.

Stacie brought the girls to the hospital, which was exactly what I needed. I saw by the look on their faces that they were terrified when they walked into Demarion's room. They were kids. They shouldn't have to witness their baby brother with tubes and machines hooked up to him. The first thing Destini told me was, "Mommy, I didn't know they had left Bari in the car." It confirmed what I had feared: she in some way felt it was her fault that this had happened to Demarion. I assured her that was okay. "It was Mrs. Alexander who should have made sure your brother was out of the car," I explained. Not only had this hurt Demarion, but it hurt his sister, too, who now felt she had some part in this horrible incident. She explained to me that when they went to take a nap she asked the other children if they had seen Bari. No one knew where he was. Once she awoke from her nap she noticed he still wasn't on his mat, so she asked the teacher. She was told he hadn't come to daycare that day. She promised me she told the teacher he had indeed come with her that morning. That's when the teacher decided to ask the owner, and the search began.

To say that I was furious is an understatement. Deja was angry. I had never seen my ten-year-old so angry. She was angry that she wasn't there to make sure this didn't happen. She was angry that Demarion was in the state he was in. She was angry that the life she was used to had been turned upside down by one careless act. She understood the seriousness of this situation. They read a story to their brother. That was one thing they both felt made him happy. As they read the story to him, I hoped he might move or miraculously wake up, but there was nothing. Could he even hear their voices? I didn't know if my baby was even in there. I did finally leave that day to take a shower. My Aunt Sharon took me home. My car was still at my job. When I made it to the house, some of my family members were there. I could immediately tell I was in for a talk.

My house was a mess on the day Demarion had been hurt. We had just returned from a trip to Orlando three days before. I had unpacked some of our stuff, but not everything. When we left home on the morning of August 2, beds were not made, clothes had not been washed and none of the dishes had been cleaned. I knew it was going to be a problem because some of the cleanest people in my family had stayed at our house while we stayed at the hospital. When I walked in the house, it was spotless. I knew between my aunt, uncle and mother they had gone through my entire house. I really didn't want to hear what they were going to say. I cared less about how messy my house was on the day before. My baby was in the hospital fighting for his life. The house could have fallen to the ground, and I couldn't have cared less. I only wanted to focus on the state of my son. Well, that wasn't the case. I went to find clothes only to have my mother and aunt catch me in the room. They told me how disappointed they were at how I had left my house messy. I guess they assumed our house was this way on a daily basis, which it wasn't. I couldn't believe I was having this conversation at this point and time. I didn't even have the strength to give a reply. All

I could do was cry. I wasn't crying because they saw my house dirty. I was crying because I didn't care. I had three young kids, and it was more important to spend time with them. My house was clean most days. I felt there was a time and place for everything. This wasn't it. I was so upset that I called my best friend and explained what had happened. She was furious. I just needed to know I wasn't being crazy and that I wasn't going to lose my mind. It didn't take me long to get myself washed and dressed. I didn't want to be at my house. I wanted to be at the hospital.

When I returned to the hospital, I noticed the caseworker with whom I had spoken. She never said anything. She only talked to the nurses. I would see her and the detectives a few more times. Not one of them ever spoke to Tim or me. I later found out they were just making their rounds. They had basically been advised that Demarion wouldn't survive. They needed to be updated in order to build their case against the owner. We tried to make the most of the waiting room. I realized this might be our home for a while. We would let the girls read, color and walk around outside every chance we could. Somehow I knew none of us would ever be the same.

I spoke with Mrs. Alexander for the first time on that day. Her husband had been calling my co-workers and friends trying to get information on Demarion's condition. It was one of the hardest phone calls I made. I didn't know what to say or how to feel. I knew in my heart she hadn't done this on purpose, but I still couldn't understand how this happened. At that point, I'm not even sure I wanted to know the details because they might fuel anger in me that I couldn't control. I called, and her husband answered the phone. The first thing he said was, "How is he?" I told him we had been told Demarion might not make it, but we were praying for a miracle. Mrs. Alexander was on the other line.

After I told him everything I knew then she spoke. The first thing she said was that she was sorry and that she never meant to hurt my baby. She was crying and upset. I knew she was sincere. She explained to me what happened that afternoon. She told me how they went to the field trip. She told me when she returned home her husband had called about windows at Lowe's, and he wanted her to see them. She explained that when she pulled up at the center she noticed trash in her yard and got out to pick up the trash. She told me how in the process of getting the trash she had told her then-14-year-old daughter to get the kids out of the SUV and into the house for lunch. She told me she then left in a different vehicle to go to Lowe's and see the windows. I listened to every detail. I realized I did need to know what happened. While it confirmed that she didn't intentionally leave my child in the car, it brought to light that she had made some poor decisions that day, which had made a life-changing event occur. She explained that Destini was looking for Demarion after her nap and that was the first time anyone noticed he was missing. Her assistant even mentioned that she had made an extra plate at lunch and didn't know why. I guess it never dawned on her to find out if there was a number discrepancy. It was hard to listen to the events that occurred while my son lay in a sweltering car for more than two hours.

She explained how they looked for him everywhere and it was her husband who suggested looking in the vehicle. Tears rolled down my face, and my heart felt like it was going to explode as I listened. She asked me how Destini was doing. The conversation was not long, but I had more details that I could share with my husband and family. At the end of the conversation I remember telling her that I knew she didn't mean to do it and at that moment I chose to forgive her. I didn't have time to hate her. My child was fighting for his life, and hating her wouldn't change a thing. It wouldn't make Demarion get out of that bed, it wouldn't make me feel better and it wouldn't help the situation at hand. When I hung up the phone I didn't really know how to feel. I was sad. I was sad for Demarion. I was sad for her and her family. I was just overwhelmed.

Chapter 5: Prayer and Faith

Now faith is the substance of things hoped for, the evidence of things not seen.

Hebrews 11:1 (KJV)

It was awful watching the doctors come in each day. They would do things to Demarion like stick him and put lights in his eyes. You name it, they did it. On the fourth day not much had changed. They couldn't keep his temperature stable. He was placed on pads that kept him freezing cold. I couldn't understand how his little body could take it. They continued to tell us his body wasn't responding to the different things they did. They said it was not looking good. One doctor wanted to prove to us that Demarion was basically gone. She told us most of his reflexes were gone, and she needed to check the reflexes of his eyes. She told us she would put the cotton in his eyes to see if he reacted. She prepared us that he would more than likely not flinch. She said this was the last reaction to go before a person dies.

I was so upset and called my parents. I let them know that they thought this might be the night Demarion would die. My parents and grandparents were having no part in this. It was pretty late, so my sister kept the girls with her at her house. My parents and grandparents rushed back to the hospital to be with Tim and me. My mother came in praying. She prayed and anointed that hospital room and told us all not to worry. The doctor got cotton balls. She pulled his eyelids open and gently placed the cotton in his eye. To her surprise he flinched. That was the first sign to me, as his mother, that we had to continue to fight for my baby. This doctor was so sure it was a fluke, she did it again. When he flinched, she just walked out. It was as if she wanted it to be over, or she wanted to prove to us that we should pull the plug on him.

Thank you, God! This was the first part of our many

prayers that would be answered. Many of the doctors thought we were more than a little crazy. They couldn't believe we continued to pray. They had seen so many children die that they didn't have faith. A few of them didn't believe in God and felt like we were being unrealistic. They believed in medicine. Everything they had learned and experienced as doctors told them this was a helpless case. As a mother, I wasn't there yet. I believed in medicine and prayer. That flinch told me to keep the faith. It told me that although this felt like more than I could handle, God would give me the strength to get through.

I didn't speak to the Alexander's every day, but I did call occasionally to update their family on his condition. On this day I wanted to talk to them about the medical expenses that we were incurring. I talked to her husband and asked him about their insurance to help with the medical bills. By this point we had been advised by doctors, social workers and others that Demarion's medical bills were adding up and any help we could get from insurance would be great. I knew it would be okay to ask because on our first meeting before we enrolled our children in the center, she told me about the insurances she had. She told us of her homeowners insurance and car insurance. Mr. Alexander gave me all of the insurance information they had, and I began to make calls to get claims started.

We also had been advised by family members and friends to obtain a lawyer. I had never retained a lawyer and didn't know where to start. So a friend gave me a few names, and I went from there. The first lawyer I called said he didn't handle those types of claims, so I moved on. The next lawyer listened to our story and set a time for a consultation. His secretary prepared us by advising us of everything we would need to bring to the meeting and what we could expect. She also advised us not to speak to the insurance adjusters any longer but to refer them to their office for further questions. Well, that was now one less thing we had to worry about.

Mrs. Alexander called to make sure we had contacted the insurance companies. I told her yes. It was time to meet with the lawyer. We didn't know what to expect when we pulled up to the office. We went in and were placed in a conference room. When the lawyer walked in, he greeted us and was very personable. He told us how sorry he was that this had happened. He then went over the case with us. We told him the details, and he told us he would represent us and discussed fees. He told us nothing would be due, and we could talk about whether we wanted him to represent us. His secretary took all of the paperwork we had brought with us and made copies.

We decided we would go with his representation and he told us he would get back with us in a day or so. He advised us not to speak to anyone about the case, not to contact an insurance adjuster or anyone else. He would now handle everything. The process felt so cold. Having no prior dealings with lawyers, I expected some four-hour meeting. This was quick and dirty. What had been discussed was factual. There would be no one disputing the facts in the case. A child had been severely injured at the hands of another person. I'm sure everyone saw this as an open and shut case. There were no major hurdles to jump over. We left feeling odd. It was odd that we even had to seek a lawyer because of what had happened. We just wanted to make sure that someone could handle the things that we had no clue about. We thought justice would be served.

The days went by. Each day seemed exactly the same. I awoke to what I now called a horrible nightmare. Each day felt like a blur. It was the same thing. I would wake up and realize yet again I was in a hospital. My baby had been hurt. He was still not responding. He was in a coma. No one could tell me when he would wake up, if he would wake up. My routine became like clockwork. The nights seemed the longest. I couldn't really sleep. It was that feeling that if I went to sleep, something would go wrong, someone would mess up. I never really slept more than three hours. I couldn't. I would wake up, look at him and pray. I would go to the main restroom, brush my teeth, wash my face and head to the chapel. I would spend a few minutes praying to God, asking for his divine favor over my son. Once I left the chapel I would walk the hall praying for all the sick children and their families. I had never been around so much hurt involving children. My eyes were sadly opened.

I would head back to the room, wash Demarion, brush his hair and try to put baby lotion all over him. This was definitely the one time I was able to brush his hair without a fuss. All I could think each day was that if he flinched at least I would know that he's still here, because he hated getting his hair brushed. There was nothing, no movement on his part, but that didn't stop me. I would then sing him all the children's songs I could think of. I would read a chapter or two from his children's Bible and ask him questions. Most of the nurses just watched as I attended my baby. We had been there long enough that they knew what I would do. Once I was finished caring for Bari for the morning my uncle would usually come in and read a few Scriptures from the Bible to him. After he would leave, most days Mr. Simp (a very close family friend) would show up with a smile and tell me to get out. He made sure I got a chance to leave and eat breakfast or just take a nice morning walk.

One cloudy day, Demarion was scheduled to have another MRI to see what was going on with the swelling in his brain. Tim had spent the night at home with the girls and came right after he got them situated. He made it just in time to see them wheel off Demarion. He sat down in the chair in the corner and seemed so angry. I can't remember exactly what we were talking about. All of a sudden he started crying. All he said was, "I don't care if I have to take care of my son for the rest of my life; I just want my son back!" It absolutely broke my heart. I had never seen my husband cry before that day. He had always been a rock. Not much got to him. I knew he was hurting, but this showed me just how much. He had such hopes and dreams for Demarion. This was his little guy. In a house full of girls, they were inseparable. Tim would plan his future in sports and brag about how tough he was. He was absolutely heartbroken over what had taken place. Nothing made him feel better. I didn't know whether he would ever be able to recover from this.

Each morning the doctors would come in, with either bad news or no news. They really had begun to make me angry. They never seemed to have faith that my son would be okay. I listened as they explained how Demarion's brain had swollen and that he had been there for a week now and the situation had not changed. By this time, in the medical field, they felt they had done all they could for him. So they rarely spoke to us. On day a doctor came into the room and advised Tim and me that not much had changed. She told us that all of the tests and scans they had done showed severe brain damage. She told us they had done all they could. She let us know that if Demarion lived he wouldn't be able to do the things he had done before. She told us that he'd basically be a vegetable and they needed to know if we wanted them to stop treating him and let him die.

I couldn't believe those words came out of her mouth. She had tears in her eyes. She was hopeless. She had no faith that anything could change. This angered me more than anything. I asked tons of questions, and she gave me the best answers she could think of. She then again asked me if we wanted them to continue to treat Demarion although they saw the outcome as pretty hopeless. Without looking at each other or even discussing it, Tim and I both replied, "Yes!" She looked at us as if she had been given the shock of her life. She angrily said, "Why would you do this to him?" I told her it was not up to me to decide this. It was up to God. There was no way we could make a decision to pull the plug on our child. We had prayed. Something kept telling me that he would pull through. I couldn't explain it, and I didn't care to even try at that point because I knew they thought we were crazy.

Tim and I knew what we could handle. We knew we couldn't live with ourselves if we pulled the plug. I had already spoken to God and told him if he was going to take Demarion home, then he would have to do it, not me. My mother was in the room with us when we were hit with this breathtaking blow. She told the doctor that she and my father supported us, and she reminded her that if God could raise Lazarus from the dead he could heal her grandson. The doctor left the room, almost in a rage. I decided I no longer had to endure the staff's hopelessness and prayed that if they were not positive that they not step foot into the room.

Tim and I left the hospital because we had planned to spend some time with the girls that night. We drove separate cars home, and I made it there first. The house was empty. The girls were at my sister's house. I walked in the house and went straight to Demarion's room. I fell on the bed and just prayed and cried my eyes out. By the time Tim made it to the house, I was a total wreck. He just sat there and tried to console me. It was that day that God told me Demarion would be okay, and we would bring him home.

My grandparents, who were in their seventies, never left our side. They, along with my parents, took over the everyday tasks with the girls. My father and stepmother would travel from Dallas and take shifts also. They kept us all together. They would make sure we ate. They would give Tim and me a break to shower and spend time outside of the hospital with the girls. They would sit with Demarion, pray over him and read the Bible to him. My Mom began playing soft Christian music in his room. If they had not been there, I'm not sure how we could have survived. To my surprise, those doctors that were negative began to stop coming in the room. They would give their medical opinion in the hall. This was just fine with me. I didn't want anything negative around my son. Now my extended family was in a spiritual fight for Demarion.

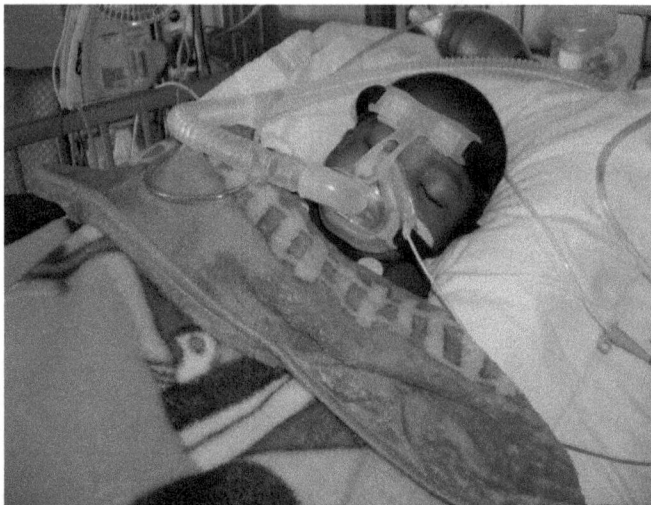

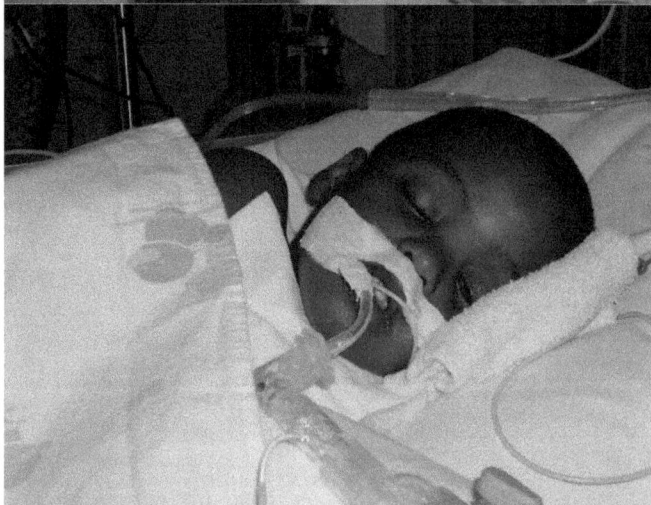

Demarion in the Pediatric ICU 2007

Chapter 6: Little Miracles

People had come from all over to see us and this little boy who was beginning to be called a miracle because he wasn't giving up. Although we had been told Demarion could only have two visitors in the room at a time, each day it seemed like the number would grow. People were waiting in the halls and waiting room to comfort us and pray for Demarion. People I had never met or hadn't seen in years began pouring in to give their support.

One Saturday, Tim and I were returning to the hospital after a night of rest at home with the girls. As we got close to the room, we noticed the room was filled with people. Of course we were not happy because the rules stated there were to be only two people in the room. My mother and about six other people were standing there talking and smiling. As we walked in, we noticed we knew some and not others. Everyone hugged us. They let us know they were praying with and for us. A little concerned about the noise level in the room, I looked for the nurse. How was I to tell these people to get out without being rude? They were there offering comfort and support. I figured a nurse could tell them better..

Well, at that moment Bari began to do something strange. The machines began to go off, and the nurse rushed in. The people in the room began to say goodbye and one man prayed as the nurses checked on Bari. After the prayer was finished, everyone but Tim and me left the room. The nurse said Demarion was having a seizure. This was the first time he had a seizure and unfortunately this wouldn't be the last. She explained that the excitement in the room might have been too much for him. We advised her that from this day forward we needed the rules to stick. If we were not at the hospital, we needed the staff to tell visitors that only two people were to be in the room at one time. She assured us that that would be the case from this point on. The only time more than two people were allowed was when our daughters came to visit. Then they allowed all four of us to stay in the room.

It now seemed like we had been in this hospital room for months. I had gone home that evening to cook dinner for the girls. Tim had stayed at the hospital with Demarion. We had begun to take shifts. Between my parents, grandparents and other close family friends someone was always at his side. Although our family was suffering, we wanted to try to keep things as normal as we could for the girls. We didn't want them at the hospital every moment of the day. Their lives had been torn apart with this whole ordeal.

When I returned to the hospital, I noticed a commotion at Demarion's room. My heart sank. I felt sick. What was going on? I saw the doctors, nurses and Tim standing over him. The doctor kept saying Bari, Bari. Oh my God, had he taken a turn for the worst? I stepped into the room, and the look on Tim's face shocked me. He almost had a smile. He looked at me and said Demarion had moved his feet. Tim explained the doctor had come in to check Demarion's eyes. When she shined the light in his eyes to see if his pupils would react, he moved. Tim said when he jumped, she jumped. Then she left the room and came back with a few things and began running things across his feet and lightly poking him, and he moved. She was shocked and told Tim it was a miracle that he was moving. She began calling his name to see if he would wake up or respond more.

This was the day I decided that Demarion was still there, and I would continue to fight for him just as he fought in that hot car on the August day. I was filled with even more hope. I felt in my heart we had made the right decision and we would see Demarion through this every step of the way. Each day seemed longer. We still had no answers. It was an awful feeling. The only thing we knew was that we would fight for Demarion. We knew that no matter what the outcome we would take care of him.

Demarion had been in the hospital for a while now. I didn't know if Mrs. Alexander would now try to come by, or if she would keep her distance. On this particular day, every one of my family members needed to get back home to take care of other things. They assured me they would be back in a day or two. God works in mysterious ways, because as soon as the room cleared, my phone rang. It was her. She wanted to come to the hospital and visit Demarion. I told her I would call her back after I talked to Tim.

I was the one who had the relationship with her . Tim hadn't spoken to her since the accident, and I wasn't sure of his feelings. I knew he realized it was an accident, but that definitely didn't stop his pain and anger. It didn't stop mine either, but for some reason I was able to deal with it. I was able to speak to them and not be overcome with anger. I talked to him, and he said he didn't care, but he didn't want to be there. He said he didn't know what he would do if he saw her, so he would leave for a while when she came. I knew I had a short window to let her visit. I knew it would be extremely hard for anyone but me to face her at this time. Emotions were high, and Demarion was still fighting for his life. I didn't want a huge scene, so I let my family know my intentions. They all agreed not to return until her visit was over.

I called Mrs. Alexander, said she could visit, and we set a time. On the day of her visit, she arrived early in the afternoon. All the nurses stayed nearby because I had told them I was allowing her to visit. While most of them didn't agree with my decision, they told me they were behind me. They too had become angry with her and the situation. They saw the pain our family was going through, and they thought it was unfair and could have been prevented. She brought her daughter and a family friend with her. I let her come into his room with me and one of his nurses. I could tell it was hard for her to see him with the tubes hooked up to him. I could only imagine what was going through her mind. She talked with me and asked if she could sing him a song. I told her that would be fine. She sang his favorite song about a turtle called Tiny Tim. She talked to him, told him she was sorry for what happened to him and said a prayer for him. Her husband called several times, so her daughter brought her the phone. Her daughter stayed in the room while she left to speak with her husband. She didn't stay very long, but it seemed like more than an hour to me.

Once she left, I called Tim and let him know she was gone, so he could return. The nurses kept telling me how they couldn't have done what I did. They didn't even want her to touch him, but I felt in my spirit that it was the right thing to do. I had no regrets letting her visit. I think I needed to see her face to face. Although I didn't have a lot to say to her, I needed to see her. I guess I needed to know she was sorry for what she had done. I felt like a huge weight had been lifted from my shoulders. If I could face her and not scream, yell or fight, I knew I was going to be okay. I knew I could keep going and continue to have faith that there was a God and that he was looking over me, watching over my son and bringing us through this situation.

August 12 was usually a fun day around our house. It was Tim's birthday. I usually had something planned, gifts and a cake. Well, the day before, my parents asked what I had planned, and I realized I had forgotten. I was sure Tim hadn't thought about it either. Each day so far had been hard to deal with. We didn't know if it was Monday or Friday. Everyone thought I should at least suggest to Tim that we go to dinner with the girls so they could celebrate their father's birthday even if he didn't want to. I mentioned it to Tim, and he didn't want to go. He'd rather spend the day at the hospital with Demarion. I told him I thought it would be good for the girls. He told me he'd do it, but he couldn't celebrate his life with his son fighting to live in a hospital. I understood how he felt. We agreed that we needed to eat and we would try to get through the day without crying.

The next day I didn't make a big deal about Tim's birthday. I told the girls we were going to take him out that evening. They were excited because it was a little time away from the hospital waiting room. My mother and grandparents kept watch over Bari while we were out. We arrived at the restaurant, and the hostess asked how many. Immediately I began to tear up, because usually it was five. Tim told her four, and I could tell he was choked up also. When we were seated and handed our menu, all I could think about was Bari. Tim looked so sad, and I knew there was nothing I could say or do to make this day better. The girls picked what they wanted, and Tim and I just ordered so that we could eat and leave. As a family, we would usually have tons to talk about, but on this day, there wasn't much conversation. Even the girls seemed a little down about going out without Bari. We made it through the dinner, and of course Tim and I needed to-go containers because we had no appetite. Once we finished, we rushed to the car and hurried back to the hospital. It just didn't feel right going anywhere without our son. I thanked Tim for doing it but told him we really couldn't do this again. It was just too hard.

There were many people that stepped in to help our family. It seemed like we were all over the place. I felt like our life had been ripped from underneath us. School would be starting in a week, and we hadn't gone school shopping or anything. To my surprise, a co-worker named Debbie called about taking the girls out for the day. I didn't know exactly what her plans were. She took the girls and bought all their school clothes, shoes and backpacks. They were thrilled. She treated them like little queens. Another co-worker, Barbara, picked them up the weekend before school started and took them to a hair salon to get their hair braided. My bosses and several co-workers brought food and many daily essentials that we might need. I was overwhelmed by the outpouring of love. I had only been at my job for about a year. Many of the people who came to our aid I had only had brief conversations with or worked with on short projects. Many teachers came to the hospital to check on our family. The girls' former teachers, the principal and office staff were regulars in the waiting room. One day my boss and his wife showed up. His wife was a teacher at the school. They showed up with bags of school supplies for our children. To our amazement, a local store heard about our situation and donated the supplies to our family on behalf of the school. These little things made this time somewhat easier.

As it became time for school to start, it was extremely crazy. Our schedule almost seemed unbearable at times. It had been three weeks since the accident. Demarion was still in a coma. We were spending all our time at the hospital. My mother, who had recently gone into remission from breast cancer, took a long leave from her job to help us with the girls. Our house was constantly filled with family members helping. Nothing seemed normal. Tim needed to go back to work. We had bills, and with both of us off work, our bills wouldn't get paid. No matter how horrible we felt, we had to make sure we had a home and utilities. Tim hadn't had his job for long. He was still in the probation period, and we didn't have much in savings…$600 to be exact. We had just taken a trip to Disney. We hadn't anticipated we'd have a life changing event happen. We felt like we didn't know what to do.

Chapter 7: Medicine and Prayer

Demarion's stats were improving, and we were told he no longer needed the ventilator. His lungs were staying clear, and he was breathing on his own. If all went as planned, he would be taken off the following day. I couldn't wait; that meant he wouldn't have so many tubes around his face. That was a huge improvement! The next morning after rounds, two nurses came in and told me the great news. The tube would be removed. I watched as they pulled the long tube from his throat, making him seem to choke. It was extremely hard to watch, but it was the most I had seen him move in weeks. They stood there and watched as he began to take breaths on his own. Their faces told me it was going well. I was so happy I couldn't cry. I just smiled and watched. They placed a mask on his face to give him oxygen. One nurse turned to me and said he was doing great. If he continued to breathe this way, he'd soon only have a small nose attachment for the oxygen. It was definitely a great morning.

Later that day, doctors advised us that we needed to make some serious decisions with Demarion. Since he was in a coma and unable to eat, they told us he needed to have a feeding tube. They also said the tubes going through his nose and mouth could have caused damage to his throat, which meant he needed a tracheotomy. I wasn't happy about either but decided that if that's what needed to be done, I would live with it. But I prayed it wouldn't come to that. I was hoping Demarion would miraculously wake up, and we'd get out of that hospital. The doctor scheduled the surgery. I researched both procedures and gathered information about care after a feeding tube and tracheotomy, but I really didn't want him to have the tracheotomy. I felt like I could handle the feeding tube, but not the tracheotomy. I asked everyone I knew to pray that this wouldn't have to be done.

Two days before the surgeries, the surgeon visited.

He spent about 20 minutes telling us everything we needed to know about the surgery and the feeding tube. Since he hadn't mentioned the tracheotomy, I asked about it. He said it wouldn't be done because the test had shown there wasn't a need for it. He apologized that no one had mentioned this to us. Demarion was breathing on his own. His oxygen levels improved, so the mask came off as well. Once the mask was removed, I could see his little face. It was so thin now. He almost didn't look like the same little boy; he was so fragile. I could see the long eyelashes and big eyes. He was still the cutest little boy I had ever laid eyes on. We were so happy. Another prayer answered.

Not long after that, one of my stepfather's co-workers came in. They told us they were not going to stay long and wouldn't make a sound. They had something to tell us and ask us. They looked at Demarion for a little while and asked if I could come out into the hall to talk to them. The ladies name was Terri. She was such a sweet lady. She told me they knew we had to be suffering financially since Tim didn't have leave to take off work. She pulled out a flyer she had made. It was asking people at the plant where she and my dad worked to please help us. She asked if she could take a picture of Demarion and add it to the flyer. At first I didn't know how to feel, but I agreed that she could take his picture since most of the tubes were off him. I had no clue what it would do, but I was touched by her willingness to help us.

A few hours later, we received a visit from another doctor. This doctor was in charge of the rehab unit of a hospital called The Children's Center. I had never heard of it, but everyone assured us this would be the next step for Demarion and that this placed worked miracles. When the doctor came for the consult, we for the first time felt like someone could give us some answers and hope. He was positive, but told us exactly what he observed. He told us he didn't know the outcome, but The Children's Center staff would work hard with Demarion. He told us we needed to set up a time to visit the hospital and meet with a caseworker to see about getting Demarion in the hospital after he was released from OU Children's Hospital.

The next morning, nurses told us we'd be moving to another room. I guessed that was great news. That meant he was doing better even though he hadn't awakened. He no longer was on the ventilator. Most of the tubes and wires were now removed. The head attending physician came to talk to us about Demarion's condition. He really had no answers. He was honest that he didn't know whether Demarion would ever wake up. The doctor told us if Demarion did wake up, he might not be able to do anything because of the internal damage done. The doctor said we would have a long hard road ahead of us caring for him if he did wake up. He told us he was sorry and basically good luck. We packed up all his things and said goodbye to the PICU.

The morning of the surgery, we were extremely nervous. None of our children had ever needed surgery. I couldn't quite wrap my mind around it; although I knew it was going to happen. I didn't sleep at all the night before. We were escorted from Demarion's room into a holding area. Everything was explained again. We met the entire team that would be working on our baby. They all assured us they would take care of him. They allowed us to stay in the holding area with him. At one point I was fooling with Demarion's blankets, some nice fleece ones that had all the Disney characters. I must have said something about holding him. The nurse came over and told me to have a seat. She said she could move all the tubes so I could hold him. I couldn't believe it. I hadn't been able to hold him since he was admitted almost a month ago. She was shocked and said it was odd that no one had let us hold him. As she moved the tubes around and placed him in my arms, he let out a sigh, as if to say, "Finally." All I could do was cry. He really knew his mommy was there. I felt it with everything in me. He relaxed totally in my arms. This was the most amazing moment. I felt the life in him. I knew he was only sleeping to allow his brain to heal. When they came to take him away, I didn't want to let him go. It was extremely hard passing him to the nurse to take away.

The surgery was only about 45 minutes, but it felt like hours. Maybe it felt like hours because we waited and waited. After more than an hour and a half, Tim and I began to become paranoid. We were told we would get a phone call in the waiting room saying when we could come to the recovery area. The phone rang several times, but it was never for us. Finally, Tim went to the recovery area and stood outside the door until it opened. When it did, he told a nurse we had been waiting. She checked and, came back and escorted us to the place where Demarion was. The nurse caring for him looked somewhat confused and worried as she worked with him. I thought, "Oh, no! What have they done to my baby during this surgery?" The nurse looked at us and said he wasn't waking up. She said she had called the doctor. We looked at her like she was crazy and almost simultaneously said, "He's in a coma!" The look of worry immediately left her face. While we were happy that he was okay, we couldn't help thinking how crazy it was that the nurse caring for him had no idea he was in a coma. It made us really worry about the care he was receiving. Thank God we were able to laugh about it a little while later. We were told he was doing fine, and they would keep him on pain medication.

We returned to his room and kept an eye on him. Several hours later, we could tell he was in horrible pain. He began to cry and moan. Obviously, his body knew how to respond to pain. It seemed like we did nothing but call the nurses and doctors in to get it under control. He would sleep for hours, but once the medication began to wear off, he would cry a horrible cry. It was nothing like anything I had ever heard. I couldn't stand it. I was angry; my husband was angry. We were told some of the pain was his brain hurting. We felt helpless. There was nothing we could do to ease his pain. The nurses turned away the visitors who came because he was in no shape to have people in the room.

It was the first week of school, which meant back-to-school night. The kids loved this night. It was a big carnival they held each year. Families came and joined in on tons of fun. There were inflatables, face painting stations, a dunk tank and cotton candy. Demarion loved back-to-school night. He would eat until he was almost sick and get his face painted. He loved to swing on the preschool playground. Well, this year, I wasn't sure if we'd even go. Demarion had just had surgery the day before. They had placed a feeding tube to his stomach. He had been in some pain, and I wasn't comfortable leaving him. Tim assured me he had everything under control and said the girls deserved to go and have some fun.

So I took the girls and was overwhelmed with the outpouring of love and concern for our family. This didn't overshadow the fun the girls had. They ate cotton candy, and Destini was adamant about taking cotton candy for her brother back to the hospital. She didn't quite understand that he couldn't eat it. He hadn't even completely come out of a coma. All she knew was Demarion loved cotton candy, and she wanted him to have it. I could see how happy the girls were just to be kids and see their friends. They had smiles on their faces, and that made the evening so much better for me.

When we returned to the hospital, I was furious. My child was in the room almost screaming. He was in excruciating pain. My husband looked as if he had been in a war. He didn't know what to do. He was at Demarion's bed trying to console him, but it wasn't working. I asked him whether he had contacted the nurse. He said he did, but she told him she would have to locate an RN who could administer his pain medication. I asked how long ago that had been. My husband told me it had been about 20 minutes. I couldn't believe they had let my child cry like this for so long. Tim assured me he called them again, but no one came in. I immediately left the room and headed to the nurse's station. When I arrived at the desk, I went off, to put it mildly. I no longer wanted to deal with the nurses. I was bothered that there were three of them sitting there, and no one had come in. The blame was passed to others, but at that point I didn't care. I blamed them all. I advised them I would be filing a complaint and someone better get a doctor or RN in the room to give my son the medication. Immediately a nurse followed me and gave him the medication, and he calmed down and fell asleep within minutes.

I was angry with my husband for not doing more. This poor man didn't even argue with me or say a word. I think he had been traumatized enough. He was so worn out, he didn't even try to plead his case. All he knew was Demarion was not hurting and that was all he wanted. Of course I got over being mad at him because I could tell he was hurt and just didn't know what else to do since he had called them twice. My husband is a very mild mannered person. He's not the arguing type. He's calm in every situation and all of this had been a bit much. He's always tried to stay in control of his emotions because I am the total opposite. It had been a long day. I was tired and so were Tim and the girls. I could tell Tim was beyond exhausted, so I gave him his dinner and told him to take the girls home. They had school, and he had to work the next day. They said their goodbyes, and I settled on the couch for the night. In hindsight, I should have tried to sleep right away because later I wouldn't get a wink of sleep. Instead, I watched a little television because it was still early for me. The volume was so low I had to read the lips. I didn't want to disturb Demarion since he was sleeping so peacefully.

I had just started to doze off when Demarion began to move his head from side to side and moan. I jumped up and went over to the bed. I tried to comfort him, but it didn't work. Within 20 minutes, he began to cry. I couldn't do anything that helped him. I picked him up. I held him tightly. I wrapped him in a blanket, but nothing worked. The cry began to get louder. At this point, I was lost. I called the nurses' station, and a nurse came right in. She tried to console him, too, but it didn't work. She told me they couldn't give him any more medication because it was too soon. She left and I was left by myself with this crying child who I couldn't help. His cry eventually elevated to a screeching scream. I was terrified. He cried, and I cried.

Eventually a nurse came in and gave him something that calmed him, but he would wake up every two hours crying. Once he began, it didn't stop until more medication could be given. I felt worthless. He was so weak and obviously in so much pain. He didn't fall asleep until the next morning. By this time I was a nervous wreck. I didn't know what we would do if this was the state Demarion would be in for a while. I was terrified. The nurses changed shifts, and the new nurse for the day came in.

She was carrying cans of what appeared to be baby formula. She explained that this was Demarion's food. This can held the key to him getting stronger. She wanted to show me how to administer it through the feeding tube, but I had to insist she leave him alone because he had just fallen asleep and I needed a break. She understood and told me she would be back in an hour to show me. Like clockwork, she came back. He was still asleep, but I let her show me how to do it. I couldn't believe this was now my life. I had heard of feeding tubes, but I had never seen one and sure never thought I'd learn how to use one! It was scary. I had to hook up a syringe to the tube and let the formula drain down the tube into his stomach. I'm not a person that likes to deal with bodily fluids, needles or anything dealing with hospitals and sick people. I don't have the stomach for it. I was just fine appreciating the people who were able to do it, and I commended them.

Now, I would basically be a full-time nurse, and I was up for the challenge. Although I was nervous, I jumped right in and did it. It was funny that I never even flinched or gagged like I might have done otherwise. We only gave him half the can to make sure he could handle it. That formula must have been what he needed because he slept for five more hours. I hadn't realized that he hadn't had food or anything with substance in weeks. Later that day, they brought in a feeding pump. This machine could administer the formula to Demarion at a slower rate and could be used at night to keep up his feeding schedule. Tim and I were given a tutorial on how to use it, and we now had more than one option when it came to feeding him. We were starting to learn what our new life with our new child would be like.

Chapter 8: Angels at Work

We had contacted the Children's Center and set up an appointment to view the facility. On the day of the appointment, a caseworker met with us and gave us a tour. She answered all our questions and helped us with the admissions paperwork. We knew this needed to be the next place Demarion went. It was close to our home, the faculty and staff seemed so caring and hardworking. We could have our family with us during the day. They provided meals for us. This place took the worry out of this situation. The goal was to have everyone focused solely on Demarion. The girls had a place they could play and unwind each day. We couldn't believe this place was in our city! We thought Demarion would have to be transported to Dallas for rehab. This seemed like the best fit not only for Demarion, but our entire family. The only hard part about choosing this facility was that only one person could spend the night with Demarion, so we would still be split up as a family. Although it would be hard, we all knew this was the best option, and we needed to go for it. All we needed was insurance approval, and he could be admitted.

My extended family began taking shifts again because it was so hard to keep everything going. My grandparents drove up once a week and stayed for two days each trip to give us a break. My stepmother came and would give all of us a break. She would make us all leave and spend the night with Demarion.

Bari would moan and cry often. Nurses told us these were possible signs he was coming out of the coma. His heart rate would soar, and it seemed the only thing that could calm him was us holding him. We did a lot of holding at this stage. Since he was now out of the Pediatric ICU, we were more responsible for him. Nurses were not constantly watching him. His care was left to us. Nurses administered meds and did shift check-ups. We hadn't been warned before we were moved from the PICU, so we were terrified. We still felt like we didn't know exactly what to do. We made the most of it, prayed and joined together as a family and did what we felt was right and helpful to him.

On this particular day, the attending physician came in and notified me that Demarion was scheduled for an eye exam in a clinic connected to the hospital. We thought this was odd considering he hadn't opened his eyes, but we went along with it. A nurse came in with a wheelchair and helped us transport him to the clinic. It was the first time we realized just how difficult it might be to transport him. He had a feeding tube hooked to him, and his little body was heavy and almost lifeless. With each movement and bump he moaned. We had to bring the feeding pump with us because he would be due for a feeding soon, and the tubes kept getting tangled and the wheels would get stuck. It was almost a disaster! We made it to the clinic only to find out it was packed with children. We figured with the state of our son we'd be in and out. We were wrong.

Three hours later, Demarion started to cry. It could have been because it was time for more pain medication or from the sound of crying kids, talking parents, a television or the lights. We couldn't believe this. Tim finally spoke with the office workers (who were not very understanding). They finally took us back. The ophthalmologist had no idea he was in a coma. He still performed whatever tests he could, which consisted of him shining more lights into Demarion's eyes. He told us no damage was done to Demarion's eyes. He was more concerned that we get counseling and financial compensation for what had happened to our son. He prayed with us and told us that with Demarion being in a coma, he was somewhat limited on another test he wanted to run. He told us we needed to come back for a check-up in a couple of months. We left the office hopeful that when Demarion finally opened his eyes he'd see the world as he had before.

The days in the hospital seemed.to linger on and

on. We began playing music in the room for Demarion. It seemed to calm him down at times. It seemed like we were there for months, but it was only a few weeks.

I'll never forget the morning we were released. We had no idea we were even being released that day. A nurse came in around 9:30 a.m. and said, "Do you guys want to get out of here?" While I wanted to leave, I had no idea what would happen. She told me we would be released today, so I needed to get all of Demarion's things together. She told me she'd be back in a few hours to help me with discharge paperwork and his transportation to The Children's Center. I was totally confused. I will admit I was ready for a change at this point. I was absolutely sick of this hospital, its food, its smell and its halls. I couldn't feel anything but pain when I thought about this place. It was a bittersweet feeling. I was eternally grateful for the doctors and nurses that helped my son, but this was just not a place I wanted to be. I was thankful for the therapists that showed me how to keep his limbs moving, the social workers who gave us vouchers for food and the child life department that provided music and books for me to read to him. I was ready not to walk the halls in the morning. I was ready for some normalcy at this point. I called Tim and told him this would be the day Demarion was released. Although he was just as confused as me, he was happy. He said he'd be there in an hour or so to help. I packed all of the cards, bears, book and blankets Demarion had. I put everything into a couple of bags that the nurse had given me and waited. No more than 30 minutes passed, and the nurse came back with discharge papers.

I explained that I needed to call my husband because we didn't have a car seat in my car. I said we weren't expecting to be discharged for another couple of hours, so my husband was on his way. She then told me that Demarion couldn't be transported in a car; he had to be transported by ambulance. She said the paramedics were on their way. They came in while she was explaining the discharge process and loaded him in a bed that had a car seat attached. They told me I couldn't ride with him because it wasn't an emergency and left. I started rushing, hoping this woman would just let me go. I could have signed my life away because I didn't want to read anymore paperwork. I wanted to get to The Children's Center. I didn't want Demarion to arrive, and I am there to make sure things were okay.

I didn't know anyone at The Children's Center. They hadn't been with him the last few weeks. What if they thought he was out of a coma like the nurse in recovery after his surgery? I once again felt out of control. I quickly said yes to everything the nurse asked me and signed the discharge papers and thought, "I can read this later." I rushed to the elevator and pushed the garage button. My heart was pounding, and the elevator was packed. Why, on this particular morning was the elevator packed and everyone needed to stop on each floor? Finally, I reached the garage level and rushed to my car. I packed his things in my car and left. I called Tim and let him know what was going on, so he agreed to meet me at The Children's Center. To my surprise, I made it to there before Demarion. The caseworker was waiting for me when I arrived. She showed me the room Demarion would have. She went over rules for the hospital and had me sign more paperwork.

While waiting, I became nervous. It seemed like it was taking the ambulance an eternity to get there. What in the world could have happened on the way to this hospital? My mind was racing and so was my heart. I didn't want to seem extremely paranoid, but I needed to know where my child was! The ambulance finally arrived with my baby a few minutes later. They explained they didn't use the sirens to get there quicker because it wasn't an emergency. I remember thinking to myself, "Why didn't they mention that to me before they took off with my child?"

Tim and I were introduced to his nurse for the rest of the day. She went over several things with me. She helped me get Demarion situated and comfortable. She hooked him up to the monitors and showed me how to operate them. She left me to get unpacked. I felt so happy that we were in a new place, a place more like a home environment. Demarion's room was huge. It was not as cold as the rooms at the other hospital. I was told I could decorate the room however I wanted. They reminded me that this would be home for as long as they could help Demarion. Before we could settle in, each therapist that would be working with Demarion came to see him. They each did their initial evaluation and let me know their plans for his treatment. While I was overwhelmed, I also felt relieved. These people were here for the sole purpose of helping Demarion begin to live his life again. I began calling family and friends to let them know of the move.

Dr. Wright came in to check on Demarion. He explained how each day would work. He explained that the damage done to Demarion's brain was extensive. He left no questions unanswered. He suggested that whoever was spending the night should get a good night's rest because tomorrow the real work would begin, bright and early at 7:30 a.m.

I will never forget the joy I felt as I settled into this hospital room. I felt like Demarion had a fighting chance. I felt like this was just the beginning. The atmosphere was that of a place of miracles.

For the first time in more than a month, I felt like eating. Tim and I ordered wings, watched television and talked about what we expected from this experience. Again we found ourselves in a place of the unknown, but at that moment we had faith that everything would work out. Tim left, and I was left by myself to care for Demarion through the night. I had become used to it and knew I needed to get sleep because he hadn't been sleeping well through the night anymore. I set up my chair/bed and called it a night. I was so excited about the next day, I hardly slept. I'm sure the excitement and feeling of a different place kept me up. I didn't want to turn on the television for fear of waking Demarion, so I just sat there staring at my baby while he slept.

When I did fall asleep, I was awakened by a nurse changing and feeding him. He was now fed through a tube and had to eat every few hours just like a newborn baby. I didn't mind, and they always tried to not wake me up. I was just a light sleeper. I offered to help, and the nurse kindly told me, "It's okay. You need your rest." I should have listened. Bright and early the next morning, I could hear the nurses and therapists talking. I looked at the clock, and it was 7 a.m. I jumped off of the chair and ran to the bathroom to take a shower. I didn't want to be the reason Demarion was late for his first therapist. I rushed through my shower, got dressed and then focused on getting Demarion washed and changed. He was now able to wear his own clothes and shoes, so I was excited to get him dressed. I had no idea what I was in for.

This simple task was now so hard. He couldn't hold himself up. His arms wouldn't move without him crying out. I did not want to hurt my baby. I was so frustrated I just started crying. All I wanted to do was get him dressed for the day, and it was horrible. He was so fragile. He hadn't slept much through the night, so he cried as I tried to do my best. I was so afraid of hurting him, but he had to be dressed. I managed to get his shorts, socks and shoes on. As I was getting his shirt on, in walks John.

John was the kind of person you never forget. He came right in and got to work. He showed me how to sit Demarion up and get his shirt on. He worked right through Demarion whining. I didn't know whether to be happy or scared. He talked to Demarion like there was nothing wrong with him. He was somewhat loud and forceful. John did a few stretches with Demarion's arms and put him in his wheelchair. He told me I could come if I wanted or go get breakfast if I hadn't eaten. I had never heard of an occupational therapist, so I was curious to see what they did.

We went into the gym, and he began to move Demarion around. With each movement he let out a cry. John would say, "Time to work Bari!" I guess he could tell I was a little nervous about all of the movement, so he began to explain each movement and why he was doing it. He explained that Bari needed to begin to use his muscles; otherwise he would lose them. He explained that my son had to relearn everything he had ever done or had been taught. He told me nothing he was doing was hurting him, but that Demarion was uncomfortable, scared and in a newborn state. While I was heartbroken, I appreciated his honesty and hard work. He told me not to be scared to move him, make him do things like hold his head up and stretch his arms. He let me know that my willingness to help him was a huge part of his recovery. He advised me to never try to overdo it, but to try and become more comfortable with it. At that moment, I realized it would be up to me to push my baby like I never pushed anyone before.

He showed me a few things to work on when Demarion wasn't in therapy or resting. He let me try them with him watching, so I could make sure I was doing it right. The hour session seemed to go by so fast. I now felt like I could do more than hold and look at my son. I realized I wouldn't hurt him if I moved him or tried to get him to move. As we walked back to Demarion's room, I felt empowered like never before. John had given me not only more hope, but a new outlook on what my role as Demarion's mother was. I think I loved John from that day on.

We returned to the room, and I let the nurse know I

was going to the cafeteria to get breakfast. I was gone for less than ten minutes. When I entered the room, there was Lena putting Demarion in his wheelchair. She smiled and told me it was time for his first physical therapy session of the day. He had been seen by a few physical therapists in the PICU, so I had some idea of what was to come. Well, this therapy session was unlike any of the ones I had seen. She took him out of the wheelchair, put him on a ball, rolled him around and had him stand. He cried the entire time.

For more than a month, he hadn't been moved like this. He didn't like it at all. It was really the first time I began to notice him really unhappy. While I was somewhat shocked, I was also happy. His crying meant he was in there. Although my heart broke for Demarion, I knew this was necessary; I knew this had to be done. This was the beginning of his new life. After the physical therapy session, I felt like someone really cared about Demarion's future.

When we got back into the room, there was the speech therapist, Kelly, waiting for us. She was bright and full of life. I'll never forget her short blond hair and chipper attitude. She asked me a ton of questions about his eating and drinking and whether he had made any sounds since being hurt. She immediately told me he was not to be fed by mouth because of the seriousness of his condition. I was shocked because we had been giving him medication, water and even ice chips by mouth. I had no idea that he could be aspirating and getting all those things into his lungs. I had even tried to brush his teeth the night before because they hadn't been touched for more than a month in the other hospital. I really felt horrible, but she made me feel better. She explained that I had no reason to suspect any of this because I had never been in this situation before. She eased my guilt by assuring me that I had a normal child and that is what a mother of a normal child would do. It wasn't my fault but the fault of the staff at the previous facility for not explaining that Demarion's swallowing ability was no longer the same. As a matter of fact, he couldn't swallow much at all without the risk of choking.

It was so much to take in all at once, but she arranged for a machine to be delivered that allowed me to brush his teeth without any of the fluid going into his mouth. She explained that she would work to get him moving his mouth, maybe making sounds, and possibly eating and drinking again one day. Her honesty about his condition was hard to hear, but I knew she would work hard to help him. I had no idea that these people would become the most important people to Demarion and me during this time. We would see them all twice a day every day. They would try to push him harder than even I imagined. It didn't take me long to realize they were not just therapists, but angels sent to help my son in the most devastating time of his life. They made the hard decisions to push him when I was afraid to because of his condition. They would teach me what to do in the future to get him better.

Later that evening my mother brought the girls to see us. She could tell I was completely worn out. She offered to switch places with me so I could go home, but I refused. I had to be right here. I had to learn everything I could to help my son. I didn't want to miss a thing. Plus, Demarion was going to get his first bath tonight. He hadn't been bathed for more than a month. The nurse had already let me know what time she would be in to help me, and I was looking forward to it. So my mother took the girls home a little early in order to give me a little quiet time while Demarion rested. I admit, I had no clue what I was in for with his bath. I'd been bathing him since the day he was born. I had begun to let him clean himself recently and just watched to make sure he did an okay job. I knew it would be somewhat different, but wow, it was totally different.

The nurse came in about 7:45 p.m. with this huge thing that looked like a rolling bed, but made of vinyl. She helped me put Demarion in it, and we rolled him away. We entered this huge, cold room. I noticed what appeared to be a sprayer that washes dishes in a restaurant. We got him undressed, and she turned on the water. She lightly sprayed him with the warm water and told me to soap him up. The neat thing about this contraption was how the water drained out at the bottom, so water never built up on Demarion. As the water drained, I was totally embarrassed at the amount of dirt that came off of my child. I couldn't believe it! The water was brown, and I could see the dirt coming off of his body. The towel was even dirty. Demarion absolutely hated it. I believe he was scared. He didn't like it much, so the nurse told me I couldn't get all the dirt off him that night. She assured me it would take a few days before he was as clean as I wanted him to be. She helped me dry him and dress him, and we returned to our room. She was an awesome nurse. She explained that I shouldn't feel bad for how dirty he appeared. She explained that while he was at the other hospital their goal was simply to keep him alive. Their focus was not keeping him clean, groomed or looking great. She let me know that while I was here, it was their job to help me get back on track in caring for his everyday needs. They would teach me how to properly clean him since he was no longer mobile. She must have talked to me for about thirty minutes about how they would help me help him in his journey to recovery.

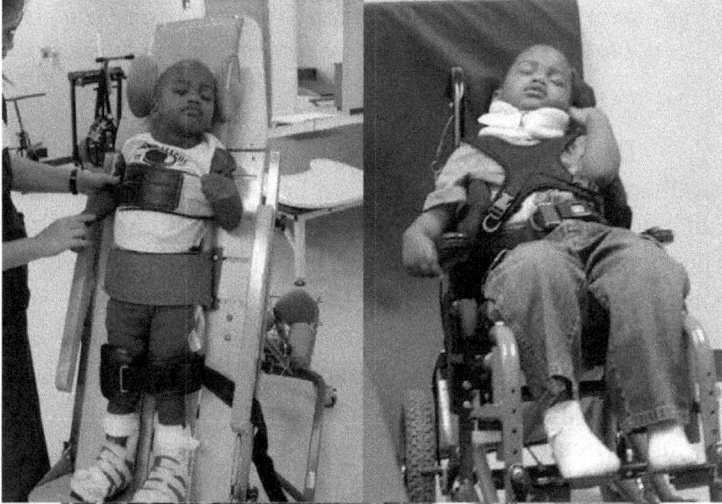

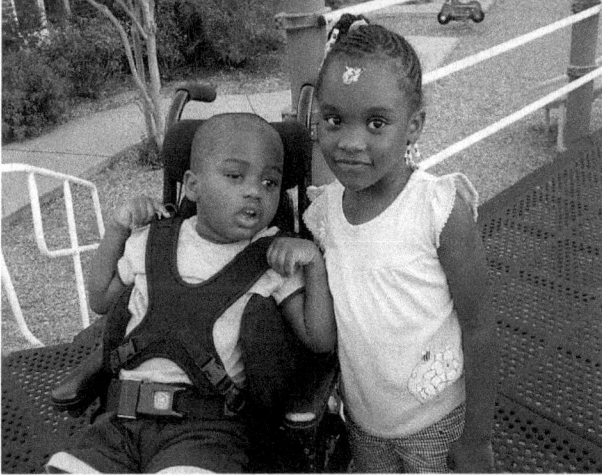

Demarion at The Children's Center

Chapter 9: New Normal

For I know the plans I have for you, plans to prosper you and
not to harm you, plans to give you hope and a future.
Jeremiah 29:11 (NIV)

Day after day, it was the same routine. Demarion had therapy all day long. He even began to have music and education therapy. I never imagined this would be our life. The therapists worked hard with him. I don't think there was one day that he didn't cry uncontrollably during therapy. Physical and occupational therapies were the worst. I was amazed at the therapists' ability to work right through it. They never stopped unless he appeared to be having difficulty breathing. The first few sessions, I was terrified. It didn't take me long to realize this was what had to be done. I realized that someday it would be me in this situation. I had to develop a tough skin, so I wouldn't give up just because he was crying. His crying was very normal. His entire body had been through something traumatic. His brain had been injured beyond any human possible repair. Most days I was sitting right there watching, taking it all in.

The days I didn't make it to therapy, I was washing clothes or had things to do with the girls. On those days, my mother, grandparents, stepmother or sometimes Tim would be there to fill me in when I returned. I soaked up all that I could during the therapy sessions. I knew that one day we would leave this place and it would be up to me to take care of Demarion by myself. I wanted him to walk, talk, eat, sit up and open his eyes. It wasn't until our second week at this hospital that he indeed did open his eyes. One evening while his sisters and cousins were playing in the room, he opened one eye. We were so excited! That one little moment gave me so much hope. The next day he opened both eyes. Although I was super excited about this improvement, I could tell he didn't seem to be looking at anything. It was just a blank stare into space. He didn't have any eye movement. At this point, all I knew was his eyes were open and that was a good thing.

Mrs. Alexander called me several times to talk and see how Demarion was doing. I would just listen most of the time. She told me how people were treating her since the accident. She was going to lose her license. She seemed to still be in shock. One day she asked me if I would write a letter on her behalf. There was going to be a hearing about what happened that day, and she needed people to tell the good about her center. I initially agreed that I could write something, because up until the day she forgot my baby in the car I hadn't had a problem. I was immediately advised against doing so. It was one thing to try to forgive her, but there was no need for me to do anything more. Although she was going to lose her license, I had lost the little boy I dropped off to her that August morning. She asked if she could bring me lunch one day, and I told her she could. She came the next day and gave me a gift card to McDonald's. She sat with Demarion and me for about 30 minutes.

As before, there was a huge elephant in the room. The therapists and nurses were appalled that she was there. They tried to be pleasant but as soon as she left, they expressed their displeasure with her being there. At this point, I didn't care. I was only concerned about my child. I didn't have time to worry about her and what was going on with her. I didn't want to be mean to her, so I dealt with her. She didn't bother me. I think I understood that she was obviously hurting, too, and if trying to see him did something for her, I was okay with it.

Over the next month, The Children's Center was my home. I even decorated Demarion's room in Sesame Street characters. I made that room his. I was so proud of what I turned the place into. It wasn't so cold. It was more inviting. There was a dvd player, and each day we played movies that he had once loved. I hoped they would spark something in him, causing him to smile or show interest.

Nothing ever happened. He never once looked at it or seemed to be interested. It was heartbreaking to realize he no longer enjoyed the things he had before. I rarely left except on Friday evenings to go home to spend the night with the girls. Tim and I were seeing less of each other. I was becoming resentful because he wasn't there as much. He was working 16-hour days and would go home only to sleep and get back up and head to work. He would come to the hospital a couple of days a week, but he called every day.

It made me so mad that one day when he showed up, I let him have it. The sad thing was I could tell just how tired and worn out he was. He had lost maybe ten pounds and looked horrible. His beard was growing, and he just looked awful. I didn't care. I was angry because he didn't make it there every day. He began asking me about Demarion's therapies, and he held Demarion and talked to him. I can't remember exactly what he said, but in my rage, I told him he didn't really care because he wasn't there each day. I have no idea why I said something like that. As soon as it came out of my mouth, I wished I hadn't said it, but it was too late. I had let my frustration, anger and lack of sleep get the best of me. I knew what I said wasn't true. I saw my husband struggle with this situation, and I knew he was torn to pieces. I had never seen Tim get so mad at me, and I've never seen him so mad at me since. The way he yelled at me let me know I had hurt him. I felt horrible, but I couldn't take it back. I tried to justify my comment, and he explained how he had to work. I wasn't working. We had two other children who had to have a roof over their heads, too. They needed food and clothing. He would not apologize for doing what he needed to as a man. We got so loud, I just knew someone would walk in the room at any time to see if we were okay. He stormed out of the room, and I knew I had been wrong. I knew I hurt him, and I was sorry.

That afternoon, I realized just how lonely and helpless Tim also felt. All he had was me and my family at this point, and I was taking my frustration out on him. He didn't have people to talk to like I did. He didn't have close friends or his blood family with him. It took me awhile, but I did call him and apologized. It took me by surprise, but he understood. He knew the stress the situation was causing. We agreed to not fight about stupid stuff, and we were fine.

By this time, my mother had moved in with us to help out. She took a leave of absence from work and stayed until she felt we could handle things. Tim had gone back to work because he had no leave. I was on an extended leave of absence from work and didn't really know the future of my career. My mother, stepmother and grandparents continued to take turns staying over the weekend to make sure I got a break. The hospital staff was so amazed that my family was so close and willing to give up their time to constantly be by our side. They would stay and sleep on the little chair that was in the room for us. My back would hurt each day when I woke up, so I knew it had to be hard on them also.

Demarion never slept through the night. It was just painful. He would cry uncontrollably for hours. The nurses would come in and try to help, but nothing really worked. I know how it made me feel, so I really felt bad when I would leave and come back the following morning to find my mom or my grandparents looking completely worn out from lack of sleep. It was hard on all of us, but it taught me more than ever that that's what family does for each other.

Word had continued to spread about the miracle of Demarion. People continued to come from all over to see him and pray with us. Many people would send food to the hospital to make sure we were all eating. Several people, churches and companies sent checks to help with our bills or other needs while we were going through this. I was overwhelmed by the outpouring of love. I didn't know that aside from the flyer Terri made that day in the PICU, there were e-mails going around about what happened to Demarion. People were so willing to step in and give whatever they could to help us get through. Words will never be able to express how thankful we were. If it had not been for those donations, we could have lost everything.

As time passed, Demarion continued the daily extensive therapies. By this time it was a given that he would be around. No one could tell us what the future held for him, but they knew he would live. His body began to adjust to all of the things he had gone through. He still had many sleepless nights and didn't perform much while in therapy. He still was unable to sit up or hold his head up on his own. He was on so much medication that I was scared they would have horrible side effects. They began giving him medication to help him sleep, which did help some.

The education therapist advised me that he needed an individual education plan for school. I honestly thought she was crazy. How could this child go to school? He was barely out of a coma. He didn't stay awake for more than a couple of hours at a time. There was nothing that anyone could teach him at this point. He was non-responsive to most of the therapies. She set up the meeting with the school officials that dealt with the children at the hospital. They came out and did an evaluation.

On the day they came, I remember trying to have everything perfect. I don't know what I was thinking. It was like he was being interviewed for the most prestigious private school, and I wanted it to go well. They were extremely nice and asked me tons of questions. The psychologist assessed his behaviors, and they left. I still had no clue what this IEP was for and why he needed it. In a few days we received the report. I learned that if he was going to go to school one day, he had to have an IEP. It set forth how they would help him learn the things he had lost. They told me he would be picked up and taken to school and while there he would get therapies, and they would begin trying to teach him basic life skills. I was amazed and happy.

I spent my 30th birthday in the hospital with Demarion. I didn't want anything but for my son to get better. This experience taught me that there were more important things than gifts. My family tried to make it a special day since it was a milestone birthday. They wanted me to stay away from the hospital and try to enjoy some free time. It didn't work. As soon as the girls were off to school, I was at the hospital. I'll never forget the look on my grandparents' faces when I walked in the room. They said, "What are you doing here? It's your birthday!" I just laughed. The only thing I wanted was to be with my baby on my birthday. A local company that did business with my mom knew about the situation. I'm positive they didn't know it was my birthday, but the owner stopped by. He was a really nice man. He brought food for us. I couldn't believe the spread. There was brisket, chicken, turkey, baked beans, green bean, potato salad and more. He brought a really nice card, too. Once he left, I opened the card, and he had enclosed a very nice-sized check to help us out. I couldn't believe how thoughtful he had been. Stacie had just had her second child, but she stopped by and gave me the cutest purse. I think that started the whole purse addiction that I have. Although it wasn't the 30th I had once hoped for, I was grateful for so many people making it a special day for me during such a hard time.

By now, school was in full swing. The girls were doing well with having something productive to do each day. Destini's preschool teacher knew all about what had happened to Demarion. She remembered seeing Demarion when the daycare center would pick up Destini each day. She was heartbroken about what happened, but she knew he would one day need to be in school. She was friends with the director of Special Services for the district. She contacted her and let her know that Demarion would need services. I remember when she contacted me. The only reason I met with her was because she knew Destini's teacher. They came to the hospital and talked to me about what they offered. I advised them that the hospital had a school come and do an IEP. They thought that was great, but Demarion didn't live in that district, so if he did come home he would need a new IEP for their district. I thought it would be at least a few months before he came home, so I wasn't worried. They gave me their information and left.

My mother's best friend would cook and send meals for us often. Her son was a therapist, and he would stop by a few times a week to check on Demarion. He would work with him and give us advice. I would tell him what they were doing, and he would let me know what he thought. It was nice to have another set of eyes and knowledge since none of us had ever gone through anything like this.

It was about three weeks in that Dr. Wright came to me and told me they hadn't seen much change in Demarion. I insisted there had been change. He was now smiling at his sisters consistently. I saw that as positive change. They had us bring in the girls so they could see whether he reacted, and of course he didn't then. I know what we saw in the evenings when the girls came to visit. I had even taken pictures of him smiling when they would say his name. The doctor advised me that we had more decisions to make. The time had come to decide what was best for Demarion.

He said we had two choices at this point. We could either leave him at The Children's Center, where he would get all of the therapies and around-the-clock care, or we could take him home. He and the social worker explained that it would be tough caring for him. They told me to take into consideration our other children. They explained that no one would think we were horrible for leaving him at the hospital. They advised me that before Tim and I made our decision that they wanted to give us a tour of the hospital side where other children who were severely disabled lived. It was explained that if we chose to leave him, he would become a ward of the state. We could still come visit him every day if we wanted. I must admit I was furious. I felt like they had given up on him. I agreed to take the tour although I knew 100% that there was no way I was leaving my child. They did tell me that if we chose to take him home, they would help us get things set up for him to have therapy and nurse care at home for a couple of hours a week.

My mind was made up. I didn't even feel like I needed to consult Tim on this matter. He was coming home. I still don't know why I went on the tour of the hospital. I think I had to see how these kids lived that had been left there. I think I was curious, because in the back of my mind I was thinking, "What if Tim and I die, and there is no one to take care of him? What will his life be like?" When they gave me the tour, I listened as we walked into the different areas. I will admit it was a nice setup, for what it was. I didn't like the big steel beds the children slept in. I didn't like that there were so many children in a room. I was devastated to say the least. My heart broke for some of those children. I had been told by a few nurses that some of their family members never came to visit. The hospital staff was now their family. Once the tour was finished, I walked back to the room with the social worker and told her there was no way he was staying. I was taking my baby home. No one would ever love him the way I did. No one would ever care for him or push him the way I could. I knew he needed to be home with his daddy and his sisters. She said she already knew my answer before we did the tour. She told me she had never seen a family like ours, and she thought I was making the right decision. It didn't make me feel any better. I was still upset that they had given up on my son. At least that's how I felt.

I immediately began to pack his things. I didn't care that we were not leaving for another week. I was ready to go right then. I had this feeling that he would get better one day, and I was determined to prove them wrong. Demarion continued his therapy over the next several days. Everyone knew we would be leaving in a few days, so they focused on showing me techniques I could use at home to help him. I couldn't help feeling like they were all feeling bad for me. Baby Bari as they all now called him was going to be a lot of work for me. I was flooded with information, suggestions, referrals and concern. The social worker set up new outside therapy for Demarion. She told me they were backed up, and it would be more than a month before they could get him in. I wasn't happy about this. What was I to do until then? He needed help! She assured me she would find therapists that could come to our home and work with him until we got in with the outpatient rehab center.

Chapter 10: A New Life

A local church heard about Demarion's story and donated money for us to purchase him a bed and bed rails. Mr. Alexander's sister met me the night before he came home and helped purchase mats, diapers and therapy balls, so I could work with him at home.

On the day we left, it was a bittersweet goodbye. I had gotten over my initial anger about having to go home. I knew what I was up against, and I was just thankful we did have the month there to adjust and learn. I left feeling confident that I would be okay. My step-dad came to the hospital that day and gave me the keys to his car. Tim and I owned a small Ford Focus, and my stepfather and mother knew there was no way we would be able to transport Demarion, his equipment and our other children in that car. It was definitely a prayer answered. We didn't have money to purchase a new vehicle, and we were just grateful.

The hospital was only about 15 minutes away from our home, but on that particular day, it seemed to take forever. We were terrified about transporting him. He had a neck brace and tons of other braces on him for stability. We drove so slowly other cars kept passing us. Once we finally made it home, it was awesome. Our entire family was there to help. Everyone wanted to make sure we would be okay. My mother chose to stay a few more days to help me get adjusted. I can't explain how much that meant to me and helped. Our girls had this look of happiness on their faces that I'll never be able to explain in words. I knew they were scared, but so happy our family was finally all together again. They jumped right in, wanting to help any way they could. They would sit on his bed and just look at him and smile. I thought that being home would be so easy. I was completely wrong. We were so nervous. Within an hour, we were visited by a nurse, companies delivering equipment and two therapists. I couldn't believe how fast everyone showed up. Demarion was set to start therapy at home the next day. The nurse showed me different techniques and shortcuts I could use by being in our home.

His first night was awful! He woke up every hour crying. His feeding machine didn't work correctly. I tried to console him. Tim and I thought we could both sleep in the bed with him to make it easier, plus we were afraid that he would stop breathing and so we wanted to be right next to him. It didn't take us long to realize that only one of us could sleep in the bed with him. We were like two brand-new parents. We got no sleep. We didn't want to wake my mom, because we knew we would need her to take over the next day so we could sleep. This would turn out to be a typical night for us for a while. Tim eventually moved out of the room and slept on the couch, so I could handle Demarion. Our house became like a convenience store. There were people in and out of the house daily. I felt like my home was no longer my home. Each day we had visits from nurses and therapists. They were all nice and extremely helpful. It was just an adjustment because I didn't know any of them, and they spent a lot of time in my home.

One day the nurse came to help me with Demarion's feeding tube. The mickey button that had been placed on his stomach seemed dirty to me, and I noticed it seemed to be leaking. When she looked at it, she told me it was no big deal; it just needed to be changed, and I needed to clean and put cream on the area. I was thinking she was going to change it, and as I waited, she looked at me. I explained that I had no idea how to do that. His tube had never been changed. She asked if I had an extra one, and I told her no. She found it odd, because it should have come with a few other things I received. I brought her everything that came in the package with the instruments needed to make the tube work, and sure enough there was a replacement. She couldn't believe no one had explained how to change the tube before we left the first hospital. I guess she felt bad that I was totally clueless and helped me out. She not only showed me how to remove the old tube, but explained how I could keep the leakage down that was causing acid to break down the skin around the tube. Once she showed me everything, she made me do each thing myself since I would be the one responsible for changing these tubes as often as they needed. I will admit, at first I was totally mortified. I couldn't stand for my children to throw up, and here I was changing feeding tubes from my son's stomach! I honestly thought I was going to be sick, not to mention the fear I had of puncturing something in his stomach. Once I did it, I knew I could do anything from this day forward. As a matter of fact, I never called a nurse to help me with any of those types of things again.

We learned to deal with our new life. Tim was back at work full time, and I didn't know what the future held for me and my job. I didn't know if I would ever go back, and at that point I didn't care. My main focus was taking care of Demarion. Things calmed down, and my mother returned home and back to work. She and my stepdad came up on weekends to give me a break. My weekdays were filled with feedings, changings, therapies, getting the girls to and from school and just taking care of everyone's daily needs. At this point, the hardest part was not knowing what to do during Demarion's crying fits. It broke my heart each day as he cried for hours. I would say it was for no reason, but obviously something bothered him. No one could tell me exactly what was going on. I would just hold him for hours, and sometimes I would cry with him. I cried because I was just as helpless as he was. I felt horrible because there was nothing I could do to help ease whatever pain was going on. Finally one of his doctors prescribed a medication that would sedate him and allow him to sleep better. While I didn't want to give it to him after I read about all of the side effects, I knew there was nothing else that might help at this point.

On the day I needed to get the prescription filled, I had no one to watch Demarion. I figured this would be easy. I would drop off the prescription and pick it up later. I loaded the loaner wheelchair in the back of the car and headed to the pharmacy. By the time I got Demarion out of the car and situated in the wheelchair, I was completely worn out. I hadn't realized this was our first actual outing or how hard it was going to be. It was worse than having a newborn. He was extremely heavy and couldn't help in any way. He had a neck brace that was bulky and in the way of all of the straps required for the wheelchair. I hadn't taken into account that his blanket didn't really work with the wheelchair. I found myself again almost in tears. This should have been a simple trip, but it wasn't. By the time I made it into the pharmacy, I was completely fragile. I could see people staring at my poor child. It made me so angry. Why would they stare and whisper? Obviously he was hurt. I guess the sight was overwhelming. I took the prescription to the counter, and the technician told me it could be filled in about ten minutes.

Well, after what I had just gone through, there was no way I was going home to return later that day. I took a seat and figured we would be just fine. I figured Demarion could handle ten minutes out. Those ten minutes passed quickly. He fell right to sleep. I imagine the ordeal of getting out of the car wore him out, too. After 15 minutes of waiting, I became a little nervous. They began calling people who arrived after us. I made my way to the counter and expressed my concern. The technician then told me I would have to speak to the pharmacist. The pharmacist explained she was concerned that a doctor would prescribe something this strong to a three-year-old. She even gave me a look as if to insinuate I was getting this for myself. She said she was waiting on a call back from the doctor. I told her that was fine, but why hadn't anyone called me to the counter to explain. She was really short with me and said she didn't know. I asked if it was going to take a long time, and she said it wouldn't. I sat and waited. As I waited, Demarion woke up. He began to cry, and I knew it wasn't going to get any better. He became louder and louder. People were staring. I was trying to console him, and nothing was working. Finally, the pharmacist called me back up and said she couldn't get the doctor on the phone, and she wasn't comfortable filling the prescription. By this time, Demarion was screaming, my nerves were shot and I just wanted the medication. She told me I would need to come back the next day. That didn't sit well with me. I was so angry! I demanded that she fill the prescription immediately. I told her I wasn't some drug addict; my child was in extreme pain. I told her that's why he was crying. She rudely said, "What's wrong with him?" Before I could think I blurted out that his damn daycare center almost killed him by leaving him in a hot van three months ago! I was in tears at this point. I told her I had just brought my baby home last week, and the brain damage was so severe the doctor knew nothing else to do but give him this medication to sedate him. I told her he was having crying fits, and no one could help me. Once she looked over the counter and saw what I was dealing with, she apologized and filled the prescription immediately. I could see the tears in her eyes. She told me she had heard about the story on the news, and she was shocked that he was alive. She told me not to worry and to make sure from now on to just have the doctor send the prescriptions over, and they would always make sure they were ready before I arrived. This wouldn't be the last time I had to deal with situations like this. Unfortunately, this became the norm in our new life. I wish I could say they always turned out this way, but they didn't.

We had been home for a few days and things, although very stressful, were more comfortable for us. Everyone was adjusting to this new change. The girls were extremely helpful and enjoying school. It wasn't long before the school district starting calling about putting Demarion in school. I will admit school was the last thing on my mind for him. I needed to get through a day without him crying for hours because his body was in pain from the trauma. I was more concerned that his feeding tube was leaking acid that was destroying his stomach. He needed therapy more than school in my mind. I wanted him to go to outpatient therapy and get back to normal!

For a couple of weeks I listened as the director of special services told me that school would be beneficial, only to be polite. Each time I hung up the phone I thought, "There is no way I'm letting him out of my sight!" He would not go to school. He didn't need to go to school. I wasn't thinking about going back to work with my child in this state. It was my mission to be with him every waking hour of the day. We were going to work on all the things he lost in the accident. At this time, school was not a part of the equation.

Chapter 11: Shocked Back to Life

I thought that dreadful day in August would be the last day I would get horrible news for a while. It had been more than a month since we first met with our lawyer. I had never needed a lawyer for anything, so when he told me not to worry and that they would handle everything, that's what I did. I didn't know what to expect, but I definitely wasn't expecting the call I received. It was October 28, 2007. I was on my way to pick up the girls from school. I received a call on my cellphone that would change my life once again. It was our lawyer's secretary. She was pleasant, but I could tell there was something wrong by her voice. She explained that they had contacted all of the insurance companies that we gave them on behalf of the daycare center. There was a huge problem that we needed to be aware of. She told me when they contacted the homeowners insurance they denied the claim for Demarion. According to the insurance company, the daycare center was not insured. The home that the center was located in was insured, but they denied the claim because there was an exclusion in the policy. The exclusion stated that if a business was run out of the home, the insurance company would not pay out any claims. I knew this sounded bad, but I figured she would follow with "but…." She didn't. She said because of this we would receive nothing from the policy. As if that weren't bad enough, she informed me they had contacted the Department of Human Services and were told that the state of Oklahoma didn't have a requirement for daycare centers to carry liability insurance. I asked her what were we to do, and she said they would look into a case against DHS, because there was nothing for which we could sue the daycare center owners.

To say I was appalled would have been an understatement. How could this happen? How could a daycare center operate without the proper insurance? How could the state license a center without requiring them to carry proper insurance? I couldn't believe what I had just been told! The assistant told me the lawyer would not charge us, because it looked like we wouldn't get much, if anything. He would do the work for free, but it didn't look good at this point. What did that mean for my son, his future, his medical cost? What would that mean for my family, our future and our livelihood? I knew the cost to care for him in the two hospitals, because I had already begun to receive bills. My insurance company had already begun to send statements letting me know he was close to his 1 million dollar lifetime maximum. I was devastated! I was angry! I called my husband, and he couldn't even speak he was so upset. What were we going to do? I had already been warned that Demarion's future medical bills would be extremely expensive. I felt like this had to be a dream! I was hoping I had been dreaming for the past few months, and I would wake up any moment. No one could handle this much bad fortune.

It took me a few days to get over the shock. It was a huge blow to what I now called my life. I didn't know what I could do, but something in my spirit told me I couldn't let this rest. I was one person. I was already overwhelmed with caring for Demarion. How could I make a change? I prayed about it. I talked to my mother about it. I thought about it until I got the courage to write an e-mail. I knew what I wanted to say, but I needed to say it so that someone would listen. I began the e-mail with what happened to my son. I figured that would get the attention of someone on the receiving end. Once I completed the last sentence, I gathered the e-mail address of every state representative in my area. I sent it to each of them individually and hit "send." I didn't know whether it could make a difference, but I had to try. I had nothing to lose by wanting to make it a requirement for a business to be properly insured. I'll never forget sitting at the computer staring at the screen hoping I would get a reply. Several minutes passed by and nothing happened, so I closed my e-mail and went about the rest of my day. I checked my e-mail each day for a couple of days with no response. I was a little bothered that no one seemed to care about what was going on. Something had to be wrong. Did they not read my son's story? Well, someone did read my son's story.

October 2, 2007, Representative Mike Shelton contacted me by e-mail. His e-mail was a simple one, "Call me." Those two words along with his office number started a journey that I will never forget. I called his office immediately, but he was not in at the time. His secretary took my information and told me she would have him give me a call. It was the next day when I got the call. I didn't realize the regular session had adjourned. No one was really at the Capitol anymore. It was definitely a blessing that Representative Shelton checked his e-mail even while he was on vacation. He had no idea who I was, but he was willing to help. He asked if I would be willing to meet with him about the issue. I couldn't believe this was happening. I was so excited, but also scared out of my mind! What was I getting myself into? I didn't know anything about getting laws passed! I soon found out it didn't matter what I knew, but that I was passionate for what I believed in.

It seemed like weeks had passed before I received a call from the local outpatient therapy center. I quickly became very comfortable with the therapist coming to my home to work with Demarion. It relieved some of the stress of having to get him out of the house. The therapist had a set time to come, and once she left I could relax for a while before it was time to get the girls from school each day. The therapist helped me become even more comfortable with Demarion. She taught me how to hold him correctly, how to make him move his legs, arms and head. She assured me I would not hurt him. Since Demarion had come home, I was always second-guessing my decisions and felt he was so fragile I might break him. My once active little boy was now like a big bag of potatoes! He seemed to weigh so much because he couldn't move on his own. The therapist helped me become comfortable with moving him throughout the house. She encouraged me to hold him up on his feet. I realized it would be up to me to help him learn that he had a body that could work again. I never imagined then just how long and slow a process it would be.

When the receptionist from the outpatient center called, she informed me they were backlogged and it would be three to four weeks before they could get him in for an evaluation. I couldn't believe it. It seemed so far away. He had already been evaluated several times. She also told me they would not be able to evaluate him for speech therapy because they were shorthanded. I was not impressed. Why couldn't he just go to The Children's Center for therapy? I knew they had outpatient services. I didn't care that this facility was closer to my home. They didn't even have enough staff to handle the people referred to them. These were all huge concerns I initially had. I set up the appointment for the evaluation for physical therapy and didn't think about it again.

It was time to meet with Representative Shelton, and I didn't know what to expect. I only knew what I wanted to accomplish and that he was willing to help. When I arrived at the Capitol, I went through security. I had Demarion with me, even though I usually avoided taking him out of the house. I knew if Rep. Shelton saw firsthand what I was dealing with, he might understand more. I brought several pictures of Demarion before the accident, so he could know what he had lost on that dreadful day in August. When I arrived at his office, I was greeted by the sweetest lady. When Rep. Shelton came out of the office, I could tell he didn't really know what to say by the look on his face. He was a very pleasant man, and his eyes told me he had a heart of gold. He asked me to follow him to a conference room. Once there, I situated Demarion and sat down. He kept offering me something to drink, but I wasn't thirsty. He talked to me about what had happened and showed so much compassion for our family. He was devastated that we had to endure such an act. He told me we would be meeting with a few people on his staff to help us get started. They had already researched the issue, and he was ready to help me hit the ground running. A few people from the research department came in and went over what they found. They had all sorts of statistics and even laws in a few other states that already required daycare center insurance. They all looked at me with such sadness, but vowed to help me help other Oklahoma families. I remember being so overwhelmed. I had no idea things could get going so fast. Was I ready for what I was about to embark on? I wasn't sure, but I knew I was here, and I was going to see it through until the very end. I was only at the Capitol for a little over an hour, but it felt like longer. When I left, I felt like I was doing something wonderful. In that moment, I felt like I was definitely doing the right thing. I felt like this horrible event truly had a bigger meaning. I felt like it wasn't the end of the world for my son or my family. I felt empowered to make change. For just a moment, I was able to see something really good come out of something so hurtful and devastating to my family.

I knew meeting with Rep. Shelton wasn't the only thing I needed to do. Our family had been devastated, and I wanted people to be aware of what could happen if things did not change in our state. I still had many friends in the broadcasting industry. I thought about who I would call to give an exclusive to. I wanted someone who knew me. I needed someone who would do this story justice. It was really a no-brainer. I immediately thought of a reporter I worked with at my last commercial television job. She was what I liked to call a bulldog. She got straight to the point, brought out the facts and had a way of telling a story that made you think. Amy was one of the best reporters I had come across. Her stories were filled with passion that struck emotion. I sent her an e-mail, told her what happened to Demarion a couple of months prior and let her know I was ready to speak about it. It didn't take her more than a couple of hours to give me a call. She knew the story, but had no idea it was my child. She was devastated and more than willing to help. She let me know she had already run the story by her news director, and they wanted it. We set a time for her to come to our house and do the story. I mentioned my goal of getting a law passed in Oklahoma, but not much more.

By this time, we were already getting tons of bills in the mail. It began to overwhelm me! I didn't want to check the mail each day because I feared there would be another bill. They were as small as $75 and as large as $3600. Where were we going to get the money? We just didn't have it. Tim was now working 18-hour days, and we were just getting by. We would always try to pay for the home health bills first, because they provided the formula for his feeding tube, the tubes and the machines that kept him fed. They provided the syringes, his suction machine and breathing equipment. With all the medication he was on, the pharmacy was the next in line for payment. I knew this would get worse before it got better. We were getting bills from the hospitals, the surgeons, and the specialists who saw Demarion. I could only do so much at this point. I began calling the offices and setting up payment arrangements.

Unfortunately, I couldn't give more than $25 dollars to each office looking for payment. At this point, all I could imagine was debt! Mountains of debt were in my future, and there would be no way I could get over it. I finally had to make the hardest decision as a mother… I would have to return to work. It was a hard decision, because my son needed me around the clock. How could I ever trust another person to watch him or any of my children at this point? I knew it was imperative that I do this, because without medical insurance or my salary we would lose everything we had worked for. A couple of weeks had passed, and we hadn't heard anything from our lawyer. I figured that couldn't be a good sign. I decided all I could do was pray about the situation, because I needed to focus on other things

Chapter 12: Demarion's Story

It was the day we were set to shoot the news story. By this time I had tons of bills piling up, and I didn't really know how to handle the situation. I got Demarion and myself together and waited for the station to show up. To my surprise, we had two other visitors instead. The two detectives who I had spoken to at the hospital the day of the accident were ringing my doorbell. They had gotten word that Demarion was released from the hospital and wanted to give us time to settle in before making a visit. They were extremely nice and sympathetic to our new situation. They shared with me what was going on with the case. I was told we might want to meet with the district attorney, because as it stood, no criminal charges were going to be filed. They informed me of the hearing that had gone on with the state that ended with Mrs. Alexander getting her childcare license revoked.

At this point, nothing really shocked me anymore. Just weeks prior, I was told there was no insurance. Before that, I was told my child would never be the same. So I definitely didn't blink an eye at this news. I didn't know how I felt about it anyhow. All I was focused on was Demarion and getting him better. I had more important things like making sure my entire family didn't crumble because of all that had gone on in the past two months. All I could do at that point was pray that God would give me strength and guide me in the direction I was to go. One of the last things one of the detectives said to me was, "Now that your son is home, the news stations will know. Don't be surprised if they start calling." Tim and I laughed, because the news station was just pulling up to our house. We told the detectives we were going to go public. They left their cards and told us to call them if we needed anything.

Amy came in, and it was like we were still working together. After a bit of small talk, I got Demarion and it was lights, camera, and action. The crew was at our house for about an hour. Amy asked the really hard questions like, "How do you feel about the woman who allowed this to happen?" She looked through the tons of bills that were stacked on my table and asked, "How can you possibly pay all these bills?" I showed her pictures of Demarion in the hospital, and she couldn't believe he was here with us today. The photographer took tons of footage of Demarion, the bills, his medications and me handling him. I could tell he was nervous because of the tubes connected to Demarion's stomach and the brace that kept his little head from falling over while he was in his wheelchair. The photographer would ask before he touched him or moved anything to get the right shot. Amy and the photographer were awesome, and the devastation of the situation showed on both their faces.

Amy wanted to know about the law I wanted to get passed. I explained that I was waiting on Rep. Shelton to get back with me after more research was conducted. I let her know that she could contact him to see if he was ready to speak on it. I remember feeling a lot better when they left. I had been able to tell someone Demarion's story. I was able to let out my feelings, my fears and what I wanted for my son's future. I had been able to speak about my frustration with the situation, and I was able to let others know this could happen to their family.

When the story aired that night, I couldn't wait to see how Amy had put it together. Our family sat by the television in anticipation. When the story was over I couldn't have been happier with my decision to let Amy tell our story. What I didn't expect was the phone calls from people I hadn't spoken to in years. The outpouring of love and compassion from friends who hadn't been to the hospital or our home because they were scared was a little overwhelming.

The following day, I received several unexpected

phone calls. The district attorney's office and our lawyer's office called. Although it might seem odd, I knew they had seen the story. At this point, my lawyer advised me to take the story to the local newspaper. He was not getting the kind of answers he wanted. He set up a day that we would give a story to a well-known reporter. I'm not sure if Rep. Shelton was hoping to somehow get us more money from the story, but all I wanted was to tell anyone who would listen what happened. I wanted all parents to know that just because their child is in a licensed daycare center doesn't mean they have insurance. I wanted families to know they could lose everything if this happened to them. I wanted them to know nothing was in place to protect them or their children. I wasn't looking for a big payday. I knew we would be stuck with the bills, and the only thing we had to depend on was our faith in God. I knew he and he alone would be the only way we could survive what was in our future.

This was the second time in my life that I knew without a doubt that I had to depend on God. The district attorney's office wanted to meet with Tim and me to let us know where they were on the case. I set up both meetings, not knowing what would come from either. I knew I didn't want anything from anyone at this point. The only thing I wanted was my little boy back. I wanted that tough little boy who kept me on my toes. I wanted the child who tested my patience and gave me a hug all at the same time. I wanted to hear his little voice say things like, "Ooh, that's nasty!" or "Hey, whatcha doing?" If I couldn't have that, nothing else mattered to me. I felt pain that was unbearable at times. There was no amount of money that would take that pain away. There was no punishment for her that would ease my fears for Demarion's future. Not one dollar could have dried the tears that fell each time my baby cried, had a seizure or had no idea who was holding him. Although I knew I had to be strong, my heart was breaking each and every day. No one could possibly prepare herself for the things we faced. I was back to changing diapers and feeding my son through a tube. We struggled to give him baths because he couldn't hold himself up. He was extremely heavy because his body was like dead weight. We could no longer do the things we liked, like going to the movies, playing music or even talking loudly. The girls no longer ran around the house being silly kids, because most noises startled Demarion, and he would begin to cry uncontrollably. Everything was out of my control, and as his mother I could only love him and pray over him.

We finally were ready to start outpatient therapy. I was super excited because this was another step in getting my son back. I didn't know what to expect, but I knew he needed it. There was only so much I could do at home, and that wasn't much, considering I was still scared to move him much. It was a cold day. I signed in and filled out a few documents for insurance and medical history. Before I knew it, a soft-spoken woman came in to get us. She introduced herself and explained that she was the physical therapist that would work with Demarion. She led us into a huge gym. She looked a little nervous, so I wasn't sure what I should think. Once we entered the room, it was even colder than outside. I noticed one of the huge windows facing a pond was broken. She explained that someone (a patient) had broken the window, and they were working to get it fixed. She said we could go into one of the rooms that had a door to get started. She must have asked me 50 questions about Demarion. I gave her the history and told her how we got to this point. I could tell by the look on her face that she was either shocked that he was still alive, or shocked that I could even talk about it. She finally finished with the questions and started moving him around. I didn't know what she was doing, and she began to explain what her initial thoughts were. I felt bad for her, because Demarion started whining. I did like that although he whined, she didn't stop. She asked if I thought he was in pain, and when I said I wasn't sure, she continued. I knew she wasn't hurting him, but she had to gauge his current abilities, which were pretty much nothing. She explained that she would see him twice a week and we set up the days and times. She also inquired about him getting other therapies and asked if I was seeing someone after her. I explained that I was told they didn't have a speech therapist or occupational therapist that could see him at the time. She told me to make sure I checked with them about the other therapies because he would need them. I will admit. She seemed nice, but I didn't know if she would be what Demarion needed. She seemed so soft-spoken. I wasn't soft-spoken. I knew Demarion needed a beast that would make him work. I had been spoiled by the therapy he received in the hospital, and that's where I wanted to be. I told myself we would give the new therapists three months, and if I didn't see any improvement, we were out of there.

Chapter 13: Therapy in many Ways

Four days later, we were back at the clinic. It seemed different. The window was fixed, and things seemed more in order. Audrey came to get us from the waiting room, and I got the shock of my life. This little woman took my son and began to work. She had him in all sorts of positions. She moved him, made him use his head and sat him up. She stretched him, bent him and made him cry. I didn't know whether to cry tears of joy or pain. Somehow I knew she would continue to be his therapist. I saw a drive and compassion that gave me great hope. Something inside me told me he had the right therapist. I left that day knowing that Audrey was just what Demarion needed. She had been the answer to my prayer.

The time was nearing for me to go back to work. I didn't want to leave Demarion. We were just getting started with therapy, and I didn't know whether my job would be willing to work with me. I knew I would most likely have to miss a lot of work because of things that involved Demarion. I spoke with my bosses, and they assured me we could figure out something that worked for all parties involved. They even advised me I could come back part-time for a while if that helped. While this made me feel somewhat better, I had another hurdle to clear. What would I do with Demarion while I was at work? There was no way on earth he was going back to a daycare center. I didn't think I could trust anyone with him or my girls ever again.

Tim worked nights and had to sleep during the day. He couldn't possibly take care of all the demands that came with taking care of Demarion and still get enough sleep. I decided it was time to send him to school. My daughters had been in the same school for years now. I knew most of the staff, and they had all been so helpful. I didn't know the special education teacher, so that made me uneasy. I had never seen her at the school. I didn't even know there was a special education program at the school until Demarion was hurt. I made the phone calls to the district and got things started. I took Demarion to the school, so I could meet the teacher before I made my final decision.

When we arrived at the school, everyone was so excited to see us. They were amazed that Demarion was still here. Many let me know they prayed for him each day. It made me feel good to know they still thought about him. The principal and office staff let me know they would all take good care of him and keep him safe while at the school. The principal took us to the classroom where Demarion would spend the day. My first impression was, "Wow, this is really neat!" Rikki Abrams, the special education teacher, had been waiting for us. She welcomed us into her classroom. She was so nice. All the assistants in the classroom loved on my baby. It was different from what I expected. It seemed like a normal classroom, with tons of adapted equipment. It was clean. The children were clean and seemed so happy. Ms. Abrams talked to me about Demarion starting, and what we had in store. She wanted to know everything about my little boy. She wrote down what he could and couldn't do, what he ate, medications he took. I felt like she not only wanted me to be comfortable, but that she and each of the assistants were there to help him reach his fullest potential… whatever that might be. I will admit, after meeting with Ms. Abrams I felt better about letting him attend school. I didn't know whether I could trust them though. I'm sure they would try to do their best, but what if something happened?

I couldn't let go of the fact that Mrs. Alexander seemed perfect, and yet Demarion almost died in her care. I knew Deja was at the school, and I even asked if she could check on him during the day. I felt that everyone was genuine, but the fear that overwhelmed me when I thought about leaving him consumed my thoughts. I told them he would start school soon, but I really didn't know when soon was. They asked if it would be next week, and I told them I would call. The next week came, and sure enough Ms. Abrams called wondering where Demarion was. I didn't have a good excuse, but I told her he wasn't starting this week. I had two more weeks before I needed to start working, and I knew I had to transition, but I didn't know how! The next week Ms. Abrams called again, "Edna, when is Demarion starting school?" I finally agreed to bring him for a couple of hours that week to see how he would do. The first day, they basically had to kick me out of the room. I think I hung around for more than an hour. They were really nice, but I could tell they wanted me to leave. When I left, I went home and cried for an hour before I returned to pick him up. To my surprise, he was just fine.

The next day, I stayed for the first hour again before I left. Once I left, I think I only cried for about 30 minutes. I did nothing but pray and watch the clock. I had no idea of the school schedule, so I kept picking him up before lunch. Each day I stayed a little less and allowed him to stay a little more. I finally let him stay for three hours the second week. Although I went home and cried each day, I still managed to leave him.

Money began to come in from all over. People at the plant where my stepfather worked showed their support by sending money to help pay for bills, food and whatever we needed it for. We received cards and well wishes from so many caring people. That money helped when my checks were short when my donated leave began to run out. It took some stress off of Tim, since he was the only one working full time. We couldn't believe how much people cared.

It was finally time for me to return to work. I explained to my boss that I could only work four hours each day. I let Ms. Abrams know that on this Monday he would be at school an entire half day. They seemed so excited that I was letting him stay. It wasn't that I was letting him. I had to. I dropped off him and his sisters that morning and made my way to work. It had been months since that horrible day that I received the phone call that changed our lives. My best friend Stacie and my managers were the only ones who knew I was returning. I think my managers didn't tell anyone in case something happened, and I couldn't make it. I told my best friend, because she had been hired to work in my office. I was so excited that she would be there. She had kept me in the loop about the changes that had taken place while I was gone.

My friend Kristy (the speed demon who got me to the hospital that dreadful day) had taken a job at a new office. We now had a new secretary. I pulled up to the center, and it felt like it was my first day all over again. I didn't know what to expect. The only person in our office I had spoken to consistently while I was away was the lead in our office. He checked on me weekly to see how Demarion and I were holding up. I walked in the door and was greeted by a new face. It was our new secretary. She was pleasant, knew who I was and told me she had heard really great things about me. Before I could get past her desk, my other two co-workers came running out of their offices in disbelief. Both said, "What are you doing here?" I explained that I was back part-time, and they gave me hugs and wanted to know how Demarion and I were. After answering a few questions, I headed to the back, where I saw the most precious sight… my best friend in the whole world standing there smiling waiting for me! Seeing her made me feel so much better. I immediately started talking to her about everything (as if we hadn't just talked hours before).

After about 30 minutes of chatting with her, I finally tried to log into my computer, but with no luck. I spent the rest of the morning getting back into my systems.

I called the school only once that day, and it was because I felt so far away from Demarion. My home was only three minutes from the school. My job was 20 minutes away. I finally got into my e-mail long enough to see that I would be overwhelmed the next day when I checked them. I had only been at work for four hours, and it was time to go get my son. I left without hesitation and got to the school. He was just fine when I arrived. He had been fed and changed, so there wasn't much for me to do when I arrived home. I couldn't believe I actually made it a half day at work with no issues. It felt good to have another outlet during the day. I didn't know how I would feel, but at the end of the day I was happy about being back at work and grateful that I had an understanding job to return to.

Chapter 14: Our First Christmas

The holidays were approaching. While we were excited that we were all home, it was hard. We couldn't travel with Demarion yet, so I had to learn to cook Thanksgiving dinner by myself. That was really an adjustment for me. I had never been responsible for everything myself. We usually spent each holiday with my mother and her family. This year all my family would be there, but us. My mother offered to come to us, but I know she wanted to see all her sisters and nieces and nephews. Plus, Demarion was not good with loud noises and crowds. I knew it would be too much for him to be around everyone. I assured her we would be fine and asked for every recipe I could think of. Debbie, my coworker, kept asking me to make her a list of things the kids wanted for Christmas because her Sunday school wanted to sponsor our family. I felt really weird about it and kept blowing her off. I kept thinking: We are not poor. I would donate to causes for poor people during the holidays, and we just didn't fit the bill, in my opinion. Finally, she called me to her office, made me sit down while she took the list. I have no idea why I was so stubborn at first. We didn't have a dime to our name. We were just getting by.

Our phone was ringing daily with bill collectors wanting their share for Demarion's medical bills. We paid what we could, paid the rent, utilities and groceries and had nothing left each month. I made it to work each day only because my stepfather gave me money each time he saw me, which I used for gas and lunch. I guess at that moment I realized that financially we were poor. It felt like we had been ruined and might never recover. I gave Debbie a small list, and she said it wasn't good enough. She began adding things she knew the girls would like and helped me search for things Demarion needed. When I left her office that day, I had no idea what would happen. Two weeks before Christmas, a co-worker called me and asked me to come to a meeting. I had no idea why I would need to go since I wasn't part of their office and I had never been to any of their meetings. The next day I showed up to what was actually a presentation. The staff presented me with a check to help with expenses. The entire division that I worked for came together and raised money to help my family. I was overwhelmed.

It was time for the school semester to end. Demarion's class had a Christmas party to attend. I didn't mind the party, but I did mind him leaving the school on a bus. His teacher tried to prepare me for three months, but it didn't help. I did not want Demarion to go. I felt that he was safe in his classroom, in his school, until I arrived each day to get him. All of the scary thoughts of that tragic day entered my mind. They had several children to look after. It was possible they would forget him just like the daycare center. Ms. Abrams assured me that if I let him go, she would call me before they left the school, when they arrived at the party and when they arrived back to the school. It took my mother to convince me to let him go. I reluctantly agreed, but was a nervous wreck the entire day until I knew he was back at school… safe.

When I picked him up, he had tons of gifts. I hadn't imagined all the wonderful things they gave him at the party. He even had a new winter coat. This was truly awesome. As I walked out of the school, the secretary stopped me. She told me to pull up to the door because they had something for our family. The church next to the school gave all three of my children a gift and our family a huge Christmas dinner basket with a turkey and all the trimmings. I couldn't believe it! The very next week Debbie called me. Christmas was now five days away. She told me to drive over to her office because she had something for me, and she needed to put it in my car. I figured it must have been heavy since I needed to drive and our offices were only about a minute walk from each other. So I drove over, and to my surprise, her entire SUV was filled with wrapped presents. My Explorer was filled with Christmas gifts for my children. They were tagged and in the prettiest gift wrap. This feeling of being overwhelmed just kept coming. I never imagined people were so good to others. I was excited as if I was a little girl again. My children had never had a Christmas like this.

When I arrived home, Tim helped me unload the gifts in disbelief. There were so many gifts that we honestly couldn't fit another one in our living room. God kept sending people right on time to help care of our needs. On Christmas Eve, I received a call from Mrs. Alexander. I had spoken with her several times since we had been home. She had given me the name of a church to contact to help us for Christmas, but Tim and I were not interested. She also told me she wanted to get the kids something for Christmas. It honestly was not a big deal to me, but it was to Tim. He didn't want anything from her. I felt that if that made her feel better, then why not accept them. Again, I was working on forgiveness. I did not want to hate her. Although she caused me more pain than I ever imagined possible, I felt bad for her. That's why I took her calls. That's why I listened to her ramble on and on, even though the conversations made me feel bad. Let's be honest, there was nothing she could ever really do to make me feel better, but I didn't want to add more hate on her.

She told me she had gifts for the kids and wondered whether it would be okay for her to drop them off. I told her yes without even thinking. Once I got off the phone I realized I hadn't spoken with Tim about it. So I went to our room and told him what I had done. I could tell he wasn't happy, but he said it was okay; he would just stay in the room when she came. He told me he was trying not to hate her, but that he could and would not be in the same room with her or her family. I totally understood. When she and her family arrived that evening, it was very awkward. When the doorbell rang, my poor husband went out the back door and stood on the porch in our backyard.

   We were all pleasant. They had gotten Demarion a wagon. They were hoping it would help us get him around. There was small talk about Christmas dinner, because her husband was a chef. As we were talking, I heard a car start. Her husband asked me where Tim was, and I didn't know what to say. I just said he was outside. Before I knew it, we heard a loud screech as if someone were speeding off. They looked at me, and I looked at them. I knew it was my husband, but I wasn't going to say it. I figured he couldn't take it, so he got in his car and left. They said bye and left. After I closed the door, I looked to see whether Tim's car was outside, and sure enough, it was gone. I was hoping he was okay, because the sound the car made let me know just how angry he was. I called him on his cell phone, and he came back to the house. He said he had to leave. He couldn't take it. He was upset. He could hear them talking in the house, and it made him angry that they were so happy and going on with their lives like nothing happened, and our son's life had been completely taken away from him. He was angry that Demarion wouldn't be able to enjoy one gift under the tree. He was hurting, and it all made sense to me.

Chapter15: A Change is Coming

I hadn't heard from our lawyer over the holidays. The New Year was here and we were just happy to have made it through 2007. I figured nothing had changed with all the horrible news we had been given, and I figured I had to live with it. I had been in contact with Rep. Shelton, and I knew what we were planning to do in the new year. I have to admit, I was shocked when I received a call from the lawyer's office. I was told that a local newspaper reporter wanted to speak with our family. I agreed to an interview, although I had no idea what more they wanted since I had done the television story. I figured I could, if nothing else, let people know what happened to my family and warn them that they could face the same fate as us.

On the day we were to meet with the reporter, I wondered how I could make an impact with the story. I knew how to tell a story; I was a reporter, but this was different. I prayed that God would guide me. I got the kids ready, and we headed to the office. Tim had to work, but he wasn't interested in doing the story. It was too much for him. He was, at this point, only filled with anger and sadness because of what had happened to our little boy. When we arrived, we were escorted to the conference room where we had initially met our lawyer. The reporter was already there. He introduced himself and expressed how sorry he was that he was writing a story because of this incident.

We must have talked for an hour. He left no stone unturned. His compassion let me know he would do an excellent story. He even interviewed the girls and got their take on things. He asked how things changed for them, how it made them feel to see Demarion in this state. While he conducted the interview, a photographer snapped pictures.

Once the interview was done, he took a few more shots to ensure he had enough. I kept thinking, "Lord, this is for a newspaper story. How many pictures could they actually print?" The reporter let me know that story would be in the Sunday paper. We said goodbye, they helped me load Demarion into the car and we went our separate ways.

The state legislature was just beginning its 52nd legislative session. Rep. Shelton called me a few times to check on our family, to give me an update and to let me know that we would definitely pursue change in this legislative session. I was excited. I was ready to take on whatever came my way. We talked about me going public with the story of daycare legislation, but he wasn't quite ready. There were a few more things that needed to be considered and thought through. I let him know I would follow his lead, but once he was ready, I would go full speed ahead.

It was a cold Saturday morning in January. Stacie needed to serve at the National Guard, so I volunteered to watch the boys for her. I was excited to have them come over, so I woke up early, and the girls and I cooked breakfast while we waited. I knew they would arrive shortly, but the phone rang. It was Stacie. I figured something must have happened, and she was running late. I picked up the phone, and I could tell she was crying. Oh my goodness, "What's wrong?" I asked. It took her a minute to answer, which made me more nervous. She said, "They have the most beautiful picture of Bari on the front page of the paper!" "What? What paper?" I asked. It was really strange to me, because the reporter told me the story would run on the front page of the Sunday paper. She told me she was at the store, and that was the first thing she saw when she walked in. She told me she was buying a few copies, and she would bring them. When she arrived at my house, sure enough, the entire front page of the paper was about my son. Our local paper printed an early edition of the Sunday paper on Saturday, and it ran on both days. I was so excited, I called my parents, and they went to the store in their town and bought several copies.

The story was more than I could have asked for. The reporter captured everything that was dear to my heart. He heard me, he heard my cry, and he let the State of Oklahoma know the injustice that had been done to my son. He told how I planned to make a change. My daughters were excited that they were on the front page of the paper and were quoted in the story. That was important, because readers got a glimpse of our lives now, through my children's eyes. The picture the photographer used of Demarion told his story. I knew this story would have an impact, but I didn't realize just how much. The next day we decided to visit a church, and as soon as we walked in, people began asking me if we were the family on the front page of the paper.

Love poured in from all over. I received so many calls from people that day. Some were good and others were ridiculous. My sister even received a few calls. One in particular was from a woman who had kept my children before. She was upset that my sister didn't tell her about the story ahead of time because one of my quotes stated that I had taken my children out of other centers for much less. I appreciated the love and concern, and I ignored the negative. I realized that in this tragedy, I was to do something more. Again, I felt in my heart that it was not about me, it wasn't about Demarion, and it wasn't about Mrs. Alexander. I was determined to make a difference.

I don't think I imagined how this story would change my life. Rep. Shelton called me and said we were going to have a full press conference about the bill he was working to get heard this session. It was named House Bill 2863. It would require daycare centers to carry liability insurance. We had several meetings about what a fair cost and coverage amount would be. We took into consideration the daycare owners and the families that used them. I wanted to make sure that families were protected, but that the cost wouldn't put good daycare centers out of business. I wasn't a legislator, so I only knew what I learned in school about the House and Senate. Going through the process takes a long time, a lot of work and a lot of guts. Once the bill was drafted, Rep. Shelton let me read it to see whether it was exactly what I wanted. While I was excited, I had one concern. I read that there would be an exemption, and I didn't like that part. I needed to know why anyone would need to be exempt. He explained that there was some push back because some daycare centers would say they couldn't afford it. The legislation would allow them to be exempt if they could show they couldn't afford it, but they had to have it posted in their center that they were not insured, so parents could make the decision. At the time I didn't like it, but I figured it was fair.

Over the next month, Demarion's name and his story were all over the news in Oklahoma. I sat in committee meetings and shared my story with legislators. I walked the halls of the Capitol and talked to as many representatives as I could, or that would listen to me. Most of them were appalled when they learned of what happened and how licensed centers weren't carrying insurance. I created a video that I sent to every representative so they could not only read the words of my story, but put a face with the name. I wanted Demarion Pittman to stick in their minds. I gave them a glimpse of the little boy who was born to my husband and me, and a gloomy view of his hospital stay, recovery and current quality of life. I worked every day to make sure people heard me, even if they didn't want to. Our first press conference was scary for me. I don't know why. I had been in the television industry for years. I knew many of the reporters and photographers, but I guess this story was so close to me, I didn't want to mess up. There were at least ten television stations waiting to question me about the possibility of the new legislation.

My mother and grandmother came to support me, and I was so grateful. It felt good to have them right by my side, smiling and supporting my every effort. In the cruel world of politics, it was nice to have people with me that I knew had my back. The questions began to come in, at first they were geared toward Rep. Shelton, and then they flooded me with them. I explained that I knew this would do nothing for my family and our current state. I knew it wouldn't help me one bit, but I hoped it would keep some other family from suffering the financial pain and strain it caused my family. Many wanted to know if I hated the woman who did this. They were curious of how we were handling things now and if Demarion would ever go to another daycare center. I was honest in all of my answers. After several minutes and more than 20 questions, Rep. Shelton ended the conference. Several of the stations asked me if they could get sound bites with me. They set up in different locations and asked me even more questions, while their photographer took more video for their station. After more than an hour of interviewing, I was worn out. I could tell my mother, grandmother and definitely Demarion were tired, too.

When the last interview was complete, we rested in Rep. Shelton's office while I fed Demarion lunch through his feeding tube. When he was finished, we walked the halls speaking with more members of the House. That evening when I returned home, my feet hurt, but I felt like I had given it my all. I had gotten at least half the members to agree to vote for the bill if it hit the House floor. We set up all the televisions in the house to record all the stories that ran on Demarion that day. His story was the top story of the day. I knew this was just the beginning because Rep. Shelton informed me that the bill had made it out of committee and would be put for a vote of the House soon. He would need me there talking to more people and sharing our story, and I was happy to do it.

As a mother, I wouldn't think of giving up. My own mother taught me to finish everything I started even if it was hard. She said it made me stronger. I recalled the summer after my senior year of high school. I had gotten a job at a tire factory in town. It was an internship, but I was put on a shift and had to sort tires. At eighteen years old, it was the hardest thing I had ever done. I had never done manual labor. I was used to babysitting. The hardest physical thing I had done before that was mow the grass and throw shot put in track. I wanted to quit after three weeks. I couldn't believe people actually applied to do this job. I honestly believed I could do anything a man could do, but I didn't even think a man should have to do this job. I would cry each day I pulled into the parking lot and each day when I left. I hated the job and begged my mom to let me quit. She would not give in; she made me stick with it. She told me one day I would look back on it and realize I could survive anything. I thought she was crazy and so mean at the time. As I thought about how at the end of the summer I was the only student that stuck it out and I had made a ton of money, I realized she was right. If I could physically survive the blisters on my feet, the calluses on my hands and the nights of no sleep, I could survive a few legislators. Each time I became nervous before I spoke or introduced myself to a lawmaker, I pulled from that experience.

Chapter 16: Demarion's Law

As the months passed, I saw Audrey push Demarion through his crying to do great things. He began to hold his head up, sit up, roll to one side and put weight on his feet. I watched her each session. I asked questions and learned what I could do at home to get him doing more. After a while, Demarion stopped crying. I have no idea when it was, because he cried every session for at least the first six months. Sometimes it was hard to listen to, but as long as Audrey pushed and he was okay, I endured it.

He eventually began speech and occupational therapies. All three of them worked hard to get him to do new things. The occupational therapist worked on getting him to use his arms and hands. We went through braces, casting and all sorts of contraptions to try to get results. He began botox injections to try to help with limb spasticity. He had arm and leg casts to help with the complications that had arisen from suffering such severe brain injury. I stressed my concern about him being dependent on a feeding tube and made his speech therapist aware that I wanted to work on him eating and drinking by mouth. She scheduled a swallow test to see where he was and whether it would be safe to start introducing things like pudding or baby foods.

Although I knew it would be a long journey, I don't think I ever realized that my son would be starting over. Each test that had been performed at this point clearly stated that he was at the stage of a newborn baby. It was a tough thing to grasp. He had a three-year-old body that did nothing that it used to. I watched these therapists repeat the same things over and over again in hopes that this day he would remember, catch on or grasp. This was definitely a slow, agonizing experience. He cried, they worked and I watched.

They were using everything they had been taught or heard about to help Demarion. This child had braces, casts, suits, shoes, and equipment to help with his new disabilities. At this point, both Tim and I were rotating days to take him to therapy. We seemed to live at the rehab center. Our daughters were growing up in this place. I became more comfortable with his therapists and the staff. These were my new people. They were the people I talked to about everything. I took mental notes of everything they did with him. His therapy didn't stop at the rehab center. I made it my mission to give him rehab at home. His room and our living room had all kinds of equipment to do daily therapy with him. I found time in between cooking dinner or helping the girls with homework. I had the most time on Saturdays and Sundays. I no longer knew what it was like to sleep in. I was up bright and early to work with Demarion, and I didn't even miss the sleep. It was my mission to never give up on him, and if I was the only one to do it, it would get done.

As I worked with him, I began to notice he never paid attention to anything. We now had toys that lit up, and I would place him in front of the mirror so he could see who he was. It was always a blank stare, as if he didn't see a thing around him. I didn't know whether it was too soon, but since his eyes were now opened, I wanted to have them checked again. I called Dr. Wright for an appointment. He was used to seeing Demarion on a pretty consistent basis now. I expressed my concerns, and he told me the possibility that Demarion might not see what he had seen before the accident. His office made an appointment with the ophthalmologist, and we were on our way. We had been informed that the waiting time was a month before Demarion could be seen. I wasn't surprised.

I was back at work full time now. Demarion was in school the whole day. Each day I went to work happy, but scared I would get a call. Each time my office phone or cell phone rang, my heart sank. I was getting ready to travel for work. I didn't want to go because it had only been six months since Demarion had been hurt. On the day I got the call about Demarion being hurt, I was two weeks out from going on this trip. My office had to cancel the training, and luckily they held my spot for a later session. In one month, I would leave my child for an entire week, and it terrified me.

In the midst of planning this trip, I was working hard at the legislature. My face was a constant in the halls. I did more news conferences, sat on panels and shared my story with anyone who would listen. I felt pretty good about the bill getting through the House. For those who opposed the bill, I sat down with them, with Demarion right next to me, and shared my story. Once they saw us face to face, they listened and changed their minds. One day, I was to share my story with a group meeting at the Capitol. Before we headed to the meeting, Rep. Shelton told me he had come up with a name for the bill. He said it had been decided it should be called Demarion's Law. They wanted to name the bill after my son. He thought it was a way to honor my child, who had unfortunately been tragically injured for this to be brought to light. My eyes filled with tears. I was not only happy, but extremely honored that Demarion would forever be a part of Oklahoma's history.

I hadn't been to the Capitol in more than a week. We had done all we could, and now it was time to wait. While I waited, I finally got new answers from our lawyer. He was working to get some sort of compensation for Demarion. He told me we would have to go before a judge to settle the case. He said the only policy coverage in place was Mrs. Alexander's car insurance. From the accident, Demarion would get $50,000 that would be put in a trust for him. While I was appalled, I figured at least he would have that one day. The lawyer also said my health insurance company could go after compensation, but had decided to waive it under the circumstances. I met with the lawyer, signed the papers in front of a judge and that was it. It didn't make me feel any kind of way. $50,000 didn't change the fact that my husband and I were in debt up to our ears behind this. It didn't change the fact that I had a little boy who was severely brain damaged and would most likely need my care for the rest of my life. I was just glad I didn't have to go back to the lawyer's office again, and I could get on with my life and work hard to get Demarion better.

It wasn't long before Demarion's Law hit the House floor. I'll never forget the day Rep. Shelton called me and said, "Listen…. Can you hear that?" I said, "What?" He said, "They are voting right now, and it looks really good!" I listened as I heard "yes" over and over. When the last vote came in, we had been victorious. Demarion's Law had passed the Oklahoma House of Representative with a 93-7 win. It was wonderful to hear. Rep. Shelton told me I did it! He was so happy and kept congratulating me. He told me this was just the first hurdle. It was now on its way to the Senate, and that would be a new ballgame. But for that moment, I was happy. In that moment, I didn't think about the work that would need to be done in the Senate. We had been victorious thus far, so I felt it would go all the way.

A few days after the law passed the House, I received a call from the district attorney's office. We scheduled a time for me to go there, and I hung up the phone. It had been months, so I figured nothing was going to happen. I didn't know what to expect. The morning of the meeting, I drove around downtown forever trying to figure out where I could park. I never spent time downtown, and I hated the one-way streets. I finally found a parking garage with a spot, although I didn't have any money. The guy gave me a ticket, and I parked. I was terrified to get out of the car because all of this was so new to me. The garage was dark, and people downtown were all rushing. I finally figured out how to exit and made it to the DA's office. I checked in with the secretary and waited for about 20 minutes before someone came to get me. It was the Assistant DA. He seemed very pleasant and kept up small talk while he led me to the conference room. He asked me if I wanted anything to drink and told me the DA would be in shortly to talk with me. I sat there in the conference room looking at all of the law books, wondering what this meeting would be about. I wished Tim were with me, but he was at work.

It seemed like that was all he did lately. This whole incident changed all the dynamics of our lives. Tim had to work overtime all the time to make sure we could make ends meet. I realized a few months prior that not only had I lost the little boy I gave birth to, but I lost his father, the man I married, too. I saw the anger and resentment building up in Tim. With each setback, he grew angrier. Each time we didn't have the money to pay a bill, I saw my quiet husband turn into a cold untrusting person. He shut down each day that he watched Demarion suffer and struggle to get some piece of his life back. All I could think about was what the news I received today would do to my husband and his current state.

A few minutes later, the DA and the Assistant DA walked in the door. I recognized him from commercials he had done during election season. He was very friendly and began talking to me about Demarion's current condition. He told me he had learned we took him home from the hospital a few months ago, and he wanted to know how our family was. He expressed that he didn't know whether I thought it was a good thing to have him home, he was glad to see me looking so well. Then it began. He started telling me about the case against Mrs. Alexander, and how his office had investigated. He told me how they were at the

hearings the Department of Human Services held. He
shared much of her testimony and the letters from other
parents who had children attending the daycare center. He
told me about the police investigation and what they had
concluded.

We must have talked for 20 minutes just about the
case. He then asked me what my husband and I were
thinking about the case. I shared with him that we didn't
know what to think. I told him since charges hadn't been
filed thus far; we figured nothing was going to happen. I
told him at that point we were not focusing on her, but on
our son. We had a little boy who will most likely need us
for the rest of our lives, and we might have to leave him on
this earth when we die to someone else to take care of. He
apologized that we had to go through this horrible ordeal,
and he expressed his sympathy for Demarion's apparent
lifelong struggles to come. He then told me that his office
had decided not to pursue charges against her because they
felt it was an accident. He then proceeded to give me a case
study on parents who had forgotten their own children in
hot cars, where they died. Those parents weren't convicted,
and he felt he shouldn't convict her of neglect because she
hadn't done it intentionally. He felt the pain she would
have to live with was punishment enough. At that moment,
I knew I had forgiven this woman, because I didn't care. As
a parent, I did feel bad that I had paid this woman, and she
harmed my child. I realized they brought me in the office
because they wanted to tell me face to face. I was just
happy there was nothing else looming over my family.
Now we could get on with our lives and try to give
Demarion the best life possible. I wouldn't have to sit in a
courtroom and relive this horrible nightmare. I wouldn't
have to testify. I could move on and take care of my
children. I figured God had a divine purpose for all of this,
and I would get through it. It wasn't for me to punish her
either. I knew in my heart she was being punished each and

every day. She had children, and as a mother, I thought about what it might do to her children if she went to jail. I thanked them for telling me face to face, and I left the office. I realized there would never really be justice for Demarion. The only way for me to deal with that was to keep fighting to get Demarion's Law passed.

Chapter 17: Seeing Us Through

As each day passed, I saw Demarion get stronger. He was beginning to stand on his feet for a few seconds at a time. He was sitting up straight and not sleeping so much during the day. These were huge improvements considering his injury and what the doctors thought might be his future. His seizures seemed to be under control, and he seemed to recognize his name. It was finally the day to see the ophthalmologist. I was so nervous. I figured it would be an all day ordeal, and I was right. It took forever for him to be seen. He was uncomfortable, and so was I. Once we finally made it to the back, they dilated his eyes and kept putting these moving objects in front of him.

They had us go back to the waiting room, and more than an hour later we were called back again. The doctor used all sorts of instruments to look into his eyes. The look on his face told me it wasn't good news. He seemed so heartbroken to deliver the news that Demarion had optic atrophy. His optic nerve had been severely damaged in the accident. While lying in that hot car and not getting blood to his brain, his eyes had in fact been affected. He explained that when the nerve fibers become damaged, they no longer send the visual signals to the brain. He wasn't sure what Demarion could see. He only knew that it was most likely blurred beyond recognition. From the look of his optic nerve, he had suffered severe vision loss. I wanted to know whether he needed glasses, and he told me glasses wouldn't help. He advised me that this was permanent, and there was no treatment or cure for it. I was heartbroken all over again. I couldn't believe what I was hearing. I didn't want to believe it. Things were starting to look so promising, and now this. How could I tell Tim? If my child were blind, this brought on a whole new set of obstacles to overcome. At this point, I wanted to crawl under a rock and die, but I just gathered our things and left. I couldn't understand why this was happening. After crying awhile, I realized I would have to get over it, and find out how we would now conquer this, too.

I had been planning my trip to Dallas for work. My hotel was booked, the class was paid in full and all of my arrangements had been approved. Demarion's teacher talked to me about a field trip the kids were having to the zoo. All I could think was not this again. He wasn't going. I would be out of town, and if anything happened, I would die if I couldn't get back fast enough. She and all the assistants assured me they would take really good care of him and that it was not fair to him to miss out on the fun. I honestly didn't care. I kept telling myself he doesn't know what's going on, so he won't miss out on any fun. She sent the permission slip home anyway and told me to seriously think about it. When I got home, all I could do was call my mom and cry about it. I did not want him to go. My mom reminded me that she would be in town caring for Demarion and so would my grandparents. She told me he would be in good hands, and they would make sure he was okay. She even said one of them would go if I wanted them to. I wish that made me feel better, but it didn't. I would be four hours away. I put the permission slip on the refrigerator and left it.

The next day Rep. Shelton called me. He had a senator who wanted to put Demarion's Law before the Senate. He wanted me to meet her. He also had been informed there was a great deal of opposition from one particular senator who had a lot of influence. The bill was to be heard at this senator's committee meeting in a couple of days, and he didn't plan to let it out of committee, which would stop it from going to the Senate floor for a vote. He thought I should meet with the senator and share my story. I agreed to meet with him two days later. When I arrived at the Capitol that morning, it was a little chilly. I had

Demarion with me, and he was not a happy camper. Just before we were getting out of the car, he needed to be changed. I didn't know what to do, because I didn't want to take him into the building stinky. So I laid him in the car and got him fixed up. As we walked to the security counter, I could see Rep. Shelton waiting for us. We got through security with the guards being extremely nice and attentive to Demarion while they checked us over.

Our first stop was the opposing senator's office. His secretary let him know we were there, and he came right out with a huge smile and extended hand. As he looked at us, I noticed the look on his face changed when he caught sight of Demarion. He led us into his office and asked what he could do for us. I told him I wanted to share Demarion's story with him and tell him a little about why I was working to get Demarion's Law passed. He proceeded to tell me how he had voters and supporters in his district who didn't like the law. They felt it was going to put them out of business, and he had to protect his supporters and district. I let him see the video of Demarion and told him the devastation that had been caused to my son's life and our family. I explained that this law would not put anyone out of business and that was one of my first concerns also. I told him how Rep. Shelton worked hard making sure insurance could be affordable, and if for some reason a provider really couldn't afford it, they could get an exemption, but they had to inform the parents.

By the time I finished, he assured me he would support the bill. He thanked me for coming in and talking to him. He even assured me he would help get support for the bill. He told us he was on his way to the committee meeting, and the bill was on the agenda. As we left the office, we met up with the senator who was carrying the bill on the Senate side. Her name was Senator Leftwich. I had seen her on the news several times. She was extremely nice and so motivated. I knew she believed in the bill and wanted to help in any way she could. She told us the committee meeting was starting soon and we needed to be there. Once the bill was recognized, Senator Leftwich talked about the bill and introduced me. The senator I had just met with gave me a few minutes to address the committee. I was so nervous, but felt so empowered. I knew what I was fighting for was right. Ironically, they placed me right in front of a handicap sign. As I told my story, a couple of the senators wiped tears from their eyes. As I went on, I could tell my voice was getting shaky. I almost started crying, but I took a second and continued with my son's story. Once I finished, it was put to a vote, and the bill made it out of the committee. It was on its way to the full Senate for a vote. I left the Capitol that day feeling yet again, victorious. I could have walked on clouds because I was so happy. I went home, shared the news with my family and friends.

There was still something bothering me. I had that permission slip on my refrigerator. I didn't want Demarion to go, but I signed it. Everyone was on board but me. I gave it to his teacher the next day, and she was happy. They promised they would send my child home safe.
I knew I would never be completely comfortable with leaving my children again, especially Demarion. There would always be this fear in the back of my mind that something could happen if I wasn't around. I began to trust people again, but only to a certain degree. I know I will never completely trust a person with my children, and I don't know if that is right or wrong; it's just the way I feel.

I prepared for the trip, and the day came to go. My parents drove up to keep the kids for me. I was excited, because it was a week of freedom, and I would get to see several family members who lived in Texas. I was also extremely nervous, because I had to leave Tim by himself. By this time, he had lost 40 pounds, and I could see he was overall not a happy person. I didn't know how he would do with my mom there, or whether he would help out. He pretty much just stayed in the bedroom when he was home, and I couldn't bear to think what my mom would think or say. I loaded the car and kissed everyone goodbye. I knew everyone was in good hands with my mom. After all, she raised me. The drive went by so fast. I blasted my Christian music, and before I knew it I was in Texas. I checked into the hotel and called home to check on my little family. Tim was at work and my Mom assured me everyone was good. I drove around near the hotel and found the place where my training would be the next morning. After I knew my way around, I grabbed dinner and headed back to the room.

The next day, I woke up refreshed and ready to start the day. I arrived at the training site early, and to my surprise they had coffee, tea and snacks for us. The training was going well, and I received a call from the kids' school on my cellphone. We were close to break time, so I let it go to voicemail and watched the clock for the next three minutes. When it was break time, I jumped out of my chair and listened to the voicemail. It was the secretary. She wanted me to know Destini was getting star student for the month. I was so excited, but sad because the ceremony was Thursday, and I wouldn't be back. So I called my mom and let her know, and she was super excited. She said they would go and take her flowers. While in training a few hours later, my cell phone rang again, and it was the school again. This time I excused myself, because it was odd to get two phone calls in one day from them. It was the secretary again. This time she told me Demarion was being awarded star student for his class on the same day as Destini! I couldn't believe it. Both of my kids were getting an award, and I wouldn't be there. I called my mom, and she laughed. She again was excited, because they were there and would get to share this moment with the kids.

That evening I didn't feel like doing anything. I missed my family. Tim called as I was leaving training. We talked about everything going on. I told him about my first day of training, and he told me what the kids were doing. I went back to the hotel, took a shower, grabbed dinner and cried myself to sleep. I wanted to go home. I had never been away from my family like this. I was going to miss so much. I wanted to be with my husband and children.

The week continued to go well. I tried to do things to keep myself occupied in the evenings. I went shopping, visited a cousin I hadn't seen in years and had dinner with my aunt a few times. Each night I went back to the hotel room, and all I wanted was to talk to my family. I was shocked when my mom told me how Tim was helping out or, should I say, taking control. She told me how he would get the kids up and get them ready for school. He was helping keep the house clean and doing everything for Demarion. I couldn't believe it. I figured me leaving did him some good, too. It allowed him to have a chance to be in charge. I had completely taken over our lives and our family since Demarion had been hurt. I turned all the hurt, anger and grief into power, determination and persistence. I was in control of our children, their schedules, activities and all aspects of their daily lives. I was in charge of Demarion's therapies, doctor appointments, feedings and medication schedules. I was in charge of our home. I did the cooking, cleaning and paying the bills. I had to have control over something, so I guess I decided it would be our lives. I had lost control with what had happened to Demarion, and taking total control of everything else helped me cope.

Chapter 18: A Mother's Prayer
And now these three remain: faith, hope and love. But the
greatest of these is love.
1 Corinthians 13:13 (NIV)

It was now Thursday April 15, 2008. I had one more
day left for training. It had been almost eight months since
the horrible accident that changed Demarion's little life.
We had been through so much during that time. He was not
the same little boy I had given birth to almost four years
ago. He was improving, but it was slow. I didn't know the
outcome of his future, and no one could tell me. All we
could do was hope for the best.

This was the day of the star student awards
ceremony, and although I couldn't be there, I was happy
my parents and grandparents would be there to support the
kids and show them love. I had been in class all day. When
I got out, all I wanted to do was talk to Destini and see how
excited she was, and I wanted to know what Demarion did
when he got his award. I called my mom, and she told me
about Demarion totally ignoring everything and how he
seemed sleepy the entire time. Then she told me how
Destini showed up at the assembly with things on that she
hadn't left the house wearing. Destini loved headbands. I
didn't let her wear her hair down, but some of the little girls
in her class wore headbands, and she wanted to wear hers.
She had asked my mom if she could wear one that day, and
my mom told her not today. Well, when Destini went up
for her award, that was the first thing my mom noticed, and
it just tickled her. I thought it was the cutest thing.

I talked with the kids and congratulated Destini. I
was a little tired from the day of training, but I wanted to
get out and do more shopping before I headed back home
the next day. I went back to the hotel, showered and headed

right back out. I had learned my way around the town pretty well, so I had no problems getting around. I stopped at the light next to the railroad tracks down the street from the hotel. My phone rang, and I noticed it was Rep. Shelton. I hadn't heard from him in a couple of weeks. When I answered, he said "Hey, how are you?" I told him I was well and explained I was in Dallas for training. He knew the area I was in and told me about a few restaurants he had eaten at. Then he said, "Well, I sure wish you were here, because I have some good news." I knew it could only be a couple of things, either I had won a million dollars or the law had passed the Senate. He told me it had passed the Senate with an astounding full support of its members. My heart dropped. I was so excited! I wanted to leave Dallas right at that moment.

He explained that Demarion's Law would be a new law in Oklahoma. It was now on its way to the governor's desk for signature. It was going to be a reality. All the hard work, sacrifice and tears paid off. I felt I had done something positive with a situation that hurt me to my core. I felt like Demarion's life was not in vain. Although I would have given anything to avoid what happened to him, at that moment, I felt the situation made a difference. I was so excited, I couldn't shop or eat. I couldn't wait to hang up the phone, so I could call my family. I wanted to let my husband know, my daughters, my parents and my grandparents. They all took this journey with me, and stood by my side. I made my rounds of calls telling everyone the bill had passed. Our family was so happy.

As I lay in my bed that night, I thought about all the people I had spoken in front of, all the interviews I had done. I thought about how I tried to handle Mrs. Alexander with compassion. I thought about the woman I was because of all of the things my mother taught me, made me do and loved me through. I had her to thank for all of this. She was the person who believed in me when I told her I wanted to be a reporter. She encouraged me when I went out for student council, class president and lobbyist for Demarion's Law. She listened to her calling from God and was able to be the best mom for me.

The next day, I was all over the place. I wanted to get home to celebrate our family victory. I explained the entire situation to my instructor and he told me I could leave a little early that day. That afternoon when I left, I felt empowered. I had this feeling that I could survive this, that even when times were tough I would get through it. I knew I could be a good mother to not only Demarion, but my girls. I felt like I could conquer the world.

I was an hour away from home when I called to check on Demarion. This was also the day he had the zoo field trip. To my surprise, my mom told me the bus had broken down, and the kids hadn't gotten back. I couldn't believe it. I called the school wanting to know what was going on. I was so upset, because what if Demarion got hot. I was an hour away. I told my mom and the school to keep me posted. I drove so fast that last hour. I decided Demarion was never going on another field trip. I couldn't believe the bus had broken down. By the time I made it to my house, Demarion was sitting on the couch just fine. I was overjoyed to be home and hear about my families' week without me. I was happy they were all there, safe and ready to be loved on.

We were all so excited about Demarion's Law becoming a law, and we all knew we would be there the day it was signed. My parents and grandparents had a million stories to tell me about the girls and Demarion's trip to the zoo. This was a turning point for me. I knew we were making a change as a family, and something inside of me spoke to my spirit and told me things were turning around for us; we were going to be alright.

When I started this journey years ago, I had an idea of how I would be as a mother. I knew I wanted the best for my children. I wanted them to all be healthy, happy and good people. I realized that God only loaned them to me, and it was my duty to raise them the way he commanded. It seemed like it took forever to hear from Rep. Shelton about the signing ceremony. It was only a few weeks, but it felt like months. The excitement was overwhelming.

On April 22, 2008, Governor Brad Henry signed Demarion's Law. My entire family came to the ceremony. Camera crews and reporters were on hand to talk to me about what this meant to me. Besides being a mother, this was one of my greatest accomplishments. Daycare centers had to carry insurance. Oklahoma parents now had a choice. They had to be informed if their center was not properly insured. Now, through my family's struggles and heartbreak, other Oklahoma families would be at least somewhat protected. It was a great feeling.

I don't know what the future holds for Demarion, but I know God does. I know I can continue to pray for him just as my mother prayed for me as I faced "giants" in the legislature. I can encourage him to reach each goal set in front of him like my mother encouraged me to fight for what I believed in. I've learned that being a mother is so much more than providing for your children. You have to be willing to fight for children, their lives and their dreams. I am so thankful I had a mother who not only loved me unconditionally, but fought for me, prepared me and pushed into the world, while always reassuring me. In 2007 I had no idea that I would be faced with so much uncertainty and challenges. Not one day has been easy. Sometimes I feel stretched so thin, but I know I have to keep going. I still have moments when I get sad when I see other boys Demarion's age playing basketball, football, baseball or just riding their bikes. I think of the what-ifs, because I know he should be doing those things and enjoying being a kid. I can't deny that I've had days that were so hard I wanted to call Mrs. Alexander and let her know just how much our lives have changed (forever) because of her negligence. Although I made the choice to forgive her, I am definitely human. I'm so thankful that my mother taught me to be strong and face adversity with faith and prayer. Although my family faced a catastrophic loss when Demarion was forgotten in that van, we've all come out better people striving for a better life. I've learned that God does give you more than you sometimes think you can handle, but he's there to see you through the battle.

My broken heart made me stronger, increased my faith and made me an even better mother. I've watched my daughters grow into the most loving, accepting and caring individuals. His struggles have taught them to never give up. Their compassion for people is extraordinary. I've learned to find the humor in almost anything. I've learned to take the good with the bad. I realize that some days will be better than others. Demarion may be great one day and in the hospital the next. I've learned its okay to cry and maybe even break down, because eventually I know I'll pick myself up, get it together and keep moving.

Epilogue

Demarion has been nothing but a blessing to our family. Although I don't have the same little boy I gave birth too, I love him just the same. He's still non-verbal, but has begun to communicate by using pictures. He continues to laugh at things that are funny. He walks with assistance and has learned to feed himself some foods. He enjoys music and walking anywhere he can. He's awesome at ignoring you when he doesn't want to be bothered and laughs out loud at the sound of his sisters getting into trouble.

With each report whether good or bad, I will continue to fight and push him as only a mother could. If it takes my lifetime to help him achieve what God has destined for his life, it will be worth it. Watching Demarion improve and beat the odds thus far has given me the strength to keep pushing when I feel I have nothing left. His smile energizes me and makes me notice miracles each day. God put me on this earth to be a mother. That is the only thing in this life that I'm absolutely sure of. Nothing gives me greater joy.

I am only a mother. There is nothing special about me. The bond I share with each of my children is precious and comes from God. He gave me love for them that defies all explanation. When my children need me most, my love will shine brighter than the brightest star. I hope my faith will help them on life's journey guided by God's tender hand.

I pray this book inspires you to never give up. I hope you will pray and have faith with each decision in your life. Ten years ago I would have told you I would completely fall apart if something ever happened to one of my children. But being able to love Demarion, care for him and watch him grow has had an impact on my life that can never be tarnished. I can't explain the strength, but I know it's a choice. You can choose to soldier through with amazing strength. When something horrible happens in your life, it doesn't have to be the end of your life. I believe with God all things are possible. You just have to hold on to his hand and believe.

Thank You

Oklahoma City Fire and Rescue and Paramedics Thank you doesn't seem like enough! Words cannot explain how much we appreciate your hard work and dedication to our son in the most critical hour of his life. Thank you for never giving up.

OU Children's Medical Center Thank you for working so hard on Demarion. Your determination, honesty, and support will never be forgotten. Each doctor that encountered our son and did everything within their power to save him. Your knowledge and professionalism is forever appreciated. The nurses in the PICU who held our hand each and every day through the hard weeks we are grateful for your love, support, faith and professionalism.

The Children's Center Bethany You guys were the first sight of hope for our family. The level of care you provided to our son and family stays in our hearts. You will forever have a special place in our hearts. Your emotional support, prayers and care helped us prepare for our new life.

Our Family Thank you all for being there with and for us from the very moment we got the call. Thank you for traveling near and far to love and support us during such a hard time. You cried with us, prayed with us and loved us right through this situation. We will never be able to express our sincere gratitude for your unwavering love. We have been blessed by your love and support.

Our Friends Thank you for the love and support. Each phone call, text, visit and prayer really made the difference.

Kristy Cummings I will never forget the car ride. You got me there in one piece and made it quite eventful. I'll never be able to thank you enough for all of the love and support you've given me and my family.

Stacie Warner Thank you for loving me past any pain that you felt. You were the first person at the hospital to support me. You are the greatest best friend a girl could ask for.

Your love and support has gotten me through so many tough times. I cherish our friendship and thank God for you each and every day.

Rikki Abrams Thank you for being the best teacher. Demarion was truly blessed when he was placed in your class. Thank you for helping through my insecurities and trust in people. You allowed me to grow in this situation. I thank you for your guidance with Demarion's future.

The FAA Academy Thanks to all of my coworkers who have helped us in any way. I can't express how much I appreciate you all.

Jim Thorpe Outpatient Rehab Thank you for being the greatest team of therapists. We could not have made it this far without your hard work and dedication. Demarion is the boy he is today because of your belief in him. Audrey, Shanun and Jill you are truly a blessing.

Representative Mike Shelton You answered my call and never turned back. Thank you for believing in what I wanted to accomplish. Your support and hard work will never be forgotten. Because of your willingness Demarion's Law will protect Oklahoma families forever. Your friendship means the world to me.

Demarion's 1st school picture

Demarion at therapy

Demarion standing again

Demarion before the accident

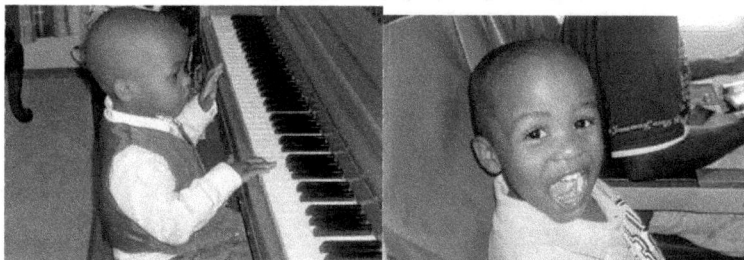

Demarion 2016